The Place of the Spirit

Princeton Theological Monograph Series

K. C. Hanson, Charles M. Collier, D. Christopher Spinks,
and Robin Parry, Series Editors

Recent volumes in the series:

Joas Adiprasetya
*An Imaginative Glimpse: The Trinity and Multiple
Religious Participations*

Anthony G. Siegrist
*Participating Witness: An Anabaptist Theology
of Baptism and the Sacramental Character of the Church*

Kin Yip Louie
*The Beauty of the Triune God:
The Theological Aesthetics of Jonathan Edwards*

Stephen M. Garrett
God's Beauty-in-Act: Participating in God's Suffering Glory

Jennifer Moberly
*The Virtue of Bonhoeffer's Ethics: A Study of Dietrich Bonhoeffer's
Ethics in Relation to Virtue Ethics*

Gerry Schoberg
*Perspectives of Jesus in the Writings of Paul: A Historical Examination
of Shared Core Commitments with a View to Determining the Extent
of Paul's Dependence on Jesus*

Anette I. Hagan
*Eternal Blessedness for All?: A Historical-Systematic Examination
of Schleiermacher's Understanding of Predestination*

Larry D. Harwood
*Denuded Devotion to Christ: The Ascetic Piety of Protestant
True Religion in the Reformation*

The Place of the Spirit

Toward a Trinitarian Theology of Location

SARAH MORICE-BRUBAKER

With a Foreword by Cyril O'Regan

☙PICKWICK *Publications* · Eugene, Oregon

THE PLACE OF THE SPIRIT
Toward a Trinitarian Theology of Location

Princeton Theological Monograph Series 197

Copyright © 2013 Sarah Morice-Brubaker. All rights reserved. Except for brief quotations in critical publications or reviews, no part of this book may be reproduced in any manner without prior written permission from the publisher. Write: Permissions, Wipf and Stock Publishers, 199 W. 8th Ave., Suite 3, Eugene, OR 97401.

Pickwick Publications
An Imprint of Wipf and Stock Publishers
199 W. 8th Ave., Suite 3
Eugene, OR 97401

www.wipfandstock.com

ISBN 13: 978-1-61097-888-0

Cataloguing-in-Publication data:

Morice-Brubaker, Sarah.

　The place of the spirit : toward a trinitarian theology of location / Sarah Morice-Brubaker ; with a foreword by Cyril O'Regan.

　xxiv + 146 pp. ; 23 cm. Includes bibliographical references.

　Princeton Theological Monograph Series 197

　ISBN 13: 978-1-61097-888-0

　1. Sacred space. 2. Place (Philosophy). I. O'regan, Cyril, 1950–. II. Title. III. Series.

BV895 .M67 2013

Manufactured in the U.S.A.

*To my husband, Phil, and my sons, Nathan and Micah:
Words cannot express my gratitude for all you've sacrificed.*

Contents

Foreword by Cyril O'Regan ix
Acknowledgments xv

1. Placing the Question 1
2. Patristic Precedents 35
3. Moltmann's Perichoretic Spaces for God and Creation 67
4. No Place for the Spirit? Jean-Luc Marion's Placial Refusal 98
5. Notes Toward a Trinitarian Theology of Place 122

Bibliography 145

Foreword

It is commonplace in forewords, prefaces, and blurbs to find the attributions of creativity and interdisciplinarity. And, as far as I can see, there is hardly an embargo on these attributions when it comes to texts in theology: the tone approving, it is often said that such and such a theological text is "creative" or "interdisciplinary" or even both. Some of these texts may very well survive scrutiny, and justify attribution, most do not: there is a significant difference between being creative and being idiosyncratic and as large a difference between mediating fully mastered areas of inquiry and collapsing different areas of inquiry into each other. I want to suggest that Sarah Morice-Brubaker's splendid new book belongs to that very special category of theology books which justifies both attributions. This is a book that puts into conversation the discipline of place studies, which is itself already interdisciplinary in that it allows under a single umbrella sociology, anthropology, human geography, and phenomenology, with contemporary theology, especially Trinitarian theology, with a view to the illumination of both. This incredibly complex operation is carried off with total aplomb and rendered in crystalline prose. If the results are probative rather than definitive, it suggests that this book is a first sounding in a remarkable fresh area of inquiry whose yield in the future is likely to be significant.

The Place of the Spirit is through and through a constructive work. It brings together a representative sample of thinkers of place, none of whom are theological in the strict sense, and asks the question whether, and if so how, this thinking can be brought productively to bear on Trinitarian thought and correspondingly whether, and if so in what way, Trinitarian thought can shed unexpected light on placial theories. Towards this end, Sarah Morice-Brubaker inserts the placial theories of Martin Heidegger and Edward Casey, Gaston Bachelard and Yi-Fu Tuan in two interlocking conversations. The first conversation is with patristic Trinitarian theology, more specifically the Trinitarian theology of the Cappadocian Fathers and Augustine; the second conversation is with the very developed Trinitarian thought of Jürgen Moltmann and with the somewhat underdeveloped

Foreword

Trinitarian thought of Jean-Luc Marion. The two conversations are interlocking in that while the patristic authors are at a relative disadvantage to their modern and post-modern successor who have available to them conceptual distinctions between 'place' and 'space' which play a central role in placial theory, Morice-Brubaker has no compunction about critically deploying figures such Basil and Augustine against either Moltmann or Marion as the need arises.

There can be no doubt that Morice-Brubaker thinks that Moltmann's Trinitarian theology, which promiscuously exploits notions of 'space,' and similarly the Christianly flavored phenomenology of Jean-Luc Marion, whose central metaphor with regard to the Trinity is that of 'distance,' have much to offer that is both experientially persuasive and theologically pertinent. This does not prevent her advancing criticisms, which are quite devasting and alone are worth the price of admission. Noting Moltmann's highly celebrated appeal to 'space' in his reflection on the relation between the Trinity and the other of creation in *Trinity and the Kingdom*, Morice-Brubaker explores whether there is a tension between Moltmann's perichoretic Trinitarian manifesto and his use of the Kabbalistic symbol of *zimsum*, God's contraction whereby a space of otherness is generated which enables God to be relational and thus, on Moltmann's view, enables God to be God. Morice-Brubaker does not criticize Moltmann for borrowing a notion from outside the Christian tradition, nor does she take Moltmann to task for making so central to his discussion of the relation between the Trinity and the world a set of spatial symbols rather than concepts. The real problem is the enigmatic origin of the activity of contraction which brings into being a 'space' of relative independence. One might have expected that it would traced back to the perichoretic relations between the persons of the Trinity, and that the role of the Spirit would be highlighted. Both of these expectations are disappointed. Thus the paradox of Moltmann's text: the overdetermination by the symbol of space and pneumatological underdetermination in which Moltmann does not account for the spacing of the divine and more specifically the placing of Spirit which is the ground of the Church. Thus, an ecclesiological deficit accompanies the pneumatological deficit. Scrupulous fair, Morice-Brubaker does not fail to track Moltmann's corrective move in *God in Creation* in which the Spirit plays a dominant role bringing God and world together in a kind of shared symbiotic energy, but unfortunately what gets lost thereby is the determinacy of the Spirit and

Foreword

its transcendent agency. Here a somewhat overdetermined pneumatology turns into its very opposite.

In the case of Marion Morice-Brubaker contends that similar deficits, that is, pneumatological and ecclesiological deficits, are arrived at by a very different path. Marion's desire in *The Idol and Distance* and other texts to prevent conceptual idolatry is approved, and his desire to exclude place from the description of God is commended. The notion of 'distance' helps to achieve both aims. At the same time it is not clear that 'distance' or 'filial distance' does not reinscribe space into the triune divine. Morice-Brubaker suggests that this reinscription might have been prevented had Marion not effectively elided the Spirit into the Son, and thus deprived the triune God of the power of placing which Basil rightly determines to be the activity of Spirit. While Morice-Brubaker is sympathetic to Marion's reasons, especially his resistance to Hegel's conflation of the Trinity in its entirety with the Holy Spirit, from a theological point of view not only is much foreclosed trinitarianly, but it becomes difficult—if next to impossible—to get a theologically satisfying view on the church. The church seems to waver between being absorbed by 'filial distance' and simply being a fact. Neither the distinction or relation of the church to the empowering divine is truly accounted for.

Throughout this book the suppleness of Morice-Brubaker's prose is married to conceptual subtlety and historical finesse. For Morice-Brubaker it is important to understand that the pneumatological deficits of Moltmann's and Marion's positions do not provide cause for pneumatological exaggeration that would displace entirely the activity of the Father and the Son. *The Place of the Spirit* does not decide in favor of the Holy Spirit as the sole agent of sanctification and indwelling, as that transcendent reality that conditions growth and meaning in dynamic life, no more than it supports or rejects Augustine's view of coinherence of the three persons in all acts that belong to and together constitute salvation history. One gets the impression that this is theological scruple more than failure of nerve, and perhaps also more a theological decision than a justified deferral. It would be easy to think here of Morice-Brubaker playing a kind of peace-maker role between Eastern and Western understanding of Trinitarian missions. What is more likely going on, however, is a mulling over such questions as to whether a decision between Eastern and Western inflections of Trinitarian missions is necessary theologically, how we are to make this decision, and what follows ecclesiologically. If only in passing, Morice-Brubaker also

Foreword

makes an important contribution to the vexed question as to whether in speaking of the Trinity we speak of the immanent and economic Trinity or solely of the economic Trinity. It must be granted that throughout *The Place of the Spirit* the focus is on the economy. It is clear that Morice-Brubaker is sensitive to the potential problem of duplication in the classical distinction, but she certainly is concerned with the tendency in the classical tradition to think of the immanent Trinity as occupying a different space to the economy Trinity. Crucially, however, in her work we are not dealing with an economic reductionism, which often supposes what it wishes to deny by insisting that we only experience God for us, never God *in se*. Here the critical realism plays in *The Place of the Spirit* a salutary role. For a Basil or an Augustine, the Trinity is economy because the Trinity is surpassingly real. It turns out that one comes to know through scripture and the light and life of faith that Trinity is also surpassingly generous: it is the activity of gift. As with the issue of the Spirit's role in the constitution of church, so also here Morice-Brubaker refuses an either-or without providing a flaccid both-and. The chapter on the Cappadocians and Augustine displays a high degree of analytic finesse. Erudition is masked by the seemingly effortless rendition of theological programs anxious to set limits to our circumscription of a divine that cannot be circumscribed. Morice-Brubaker beautifully underscores the all important reversal in which it is the triune God who circumscribes us, who places us in existence, positions our knowing, and actively locates us in the very particularity of our lives in a world that we constantly negotiate or—to use the idiom of place theory—constantly 'navigate.' If, arguably, the Cappadocians in general, and Basil in particular, do a slightly better job than Augustine, Morice-Brubaker underscores the existential power not only of Augustine's insistence on the limitations of our knowledge, but also of his fierce determination in his anti-Manichaean writings not to allow God to be associated with space. One cannot credit Morice-Brubaker enough that when she brings early Christian thought to our attention as both a productive and critical theological resource, she does not fall a hapless victim to anachronism. There are questions that the Church fathers did not ask. Our retrieval of them will necessarily involve saying more than they said; we are invested with the responsibility of developing their ideas. The good news is that there are such ideas to be developed, and in their development in and through conversation with placial thought, these figures are a match for the very best that contemporary Trinitarian thought has produced.

Foreword

The Place of the Spirit is a marvelous debut by an immensely talented young theologian of wonderful intelligence and superior writing skill. Much can be expected of Morice-Brubaker. This is book of deep and resonant sounding; more will follow. The author is completely aware of this and acknowledges it explicitly in her last chapter, and implicitly by having as the title of her last chapter," Notes toward a Trinitarian Theology of Place." If these are notes, then they are deep ones; and if this book provides no more than a map—notice the placial metaphor—the orienting capacity of such is very strong. We get a strong sense as to where the journey will lead, but remained intrigued not only because we do not see all the way, but we have learned not only to trust the author of *The Place of the Spirit*, but come to expect being surprised by invention and by having familiar constructs turned around and looking very different. We have come to expect reversal. And this is as it should be; for this is what Morice-Brubaker has been speaking about all along.

Cyril O'Regan
Huisking Professor of Theology
University of Notre Dame

Acknowledgments

GIVEN MY TOPIC, A NUMBER OF METAPHORS SUGGEST THEMSELVES HERE, all within the broad category of navigation. My doctoral adviser, Cyril O'Regan, and co-director, Gerald McKenny, have been guides, orienteering instructors, cartographers, and expedition backers. More than once they have kept me from getting hopelessly lost. In so doing they have given me a theological world, and a sense of direction with which to find my way around in it. I am so fortunate to have had mentors with their grace, knowledge, care, and kindness. And such patience! I am grateful as well for the grace, good humor, and wisdom of my committee members: J. Matthew Ashley, John Cavadini, and Mary Catherine Hilkert. They, and indeed the entire department of theology at Notre Dame, have formed me intellectually in ways I am still discovering. To them, I offer my deepest thanks.

Another theological community has been a part of this process, several states away from the chilly environs of South Bend. My colleagues at Phillips Theological Seminary have cheered me on, helped me to bounce ideas around, and made time for me to write even when it meant more work for them. Four members of the PTS community deserve special mention. First, the dean, Don Pittman, was every new faculty member's dream. He protected me from commitments that would have made writing impossible, but far more importantly he is a profoundly good person. My senior colleague in theology, Joe Bessler, was a kind, generous, and knowledgeable conversation partner and mentor. The better parts of the book bear the mark of his theological influence, and I am grateful for it. One of my student assistants, Laura West, provided the literal legwork of hunting down sources, always with her characteristic good humor and poise. Finally, I owe a tremendous debt of gratitude to Anna Holloway, a PTS alumna, who prepared the manuscript for publication. She very gently alerted me, for example, to the fact that I have a (in her words) "hyphen problem." I expect this problem persists in the finished product, despite her heroic efforts. Readers should know that this is my fault, not hers.

Acknowledgments

Many authors do not have the pleasure of working with an editor whom they first knew in another context, and I am sorry to say that those authors are missing out. A decade ago, when I was a Duke Divinity student and he a doctoral candidate in theology, I would have said that it is a delight to know Charlie Collier. Now I am able to say that it is a delight to know and work with Charlie Collier. He and his colleagues at Wipf and Stock are bringing so much good theological writing to the world, in ways that are ethical and downright inspiring. It is an honor to publish this book through them.

My parents offered immeasurable support, too much to summarize, but which included childcare and cheerleading. I have no doubt they feel relieved. I hope they feel appreciated. They are, very much so. Finally, I can find no suitable words to express my gratitude to Phil, my husband, and our children, Nathan and Micah. The sacrifices they made were not, I am well aware, always pleasant or edifying. Nobody asked them how their book was proceeding. Nobody congratulated Phil for being up all night with a sick child so that I would be able to write the next day. Whatever favor might attach to this project belongs, by rights, first to them. For now, I can only ask one more favor of them. My loves, please imagine that I have found some adequate way of expressing, here, my deepest thanks.

1

Placing the Question

Trinity and . . . Place?

IS THERE ANY THEOLOGICALLY APPROPRIATE WAY TO TALK ABOUT TRINITY and place?

Is there any way to talk about the trinity's location, while yet making all the qualifications, hedges, and provisions necessary to preserve a sense of God's otherness? Or does one who so much as whispers "location" and "trinity" in the same theological thought thereby risk committing idolatry?

This question drives the present dissertation. From one angle, the currency of the question is a function of this inquiry's particular North American academic, early twenty-first-century context. Place is a current theological (and philosophical, and sociological) topic, in the academy and in the dominant culture. Over two decades entirely new ways of being placed (e.g., in online environments) have been synthesized. In many fields—philosophy, sociology, geography, cultural studies—there is a growing consensus that "location" has to do with much more than just material, geometric extension. More broadly, at least in the more privileged cultural pockets of first-world economies, one finds as well a persistent nostalgia for location—understood to mean rootedness, a tie to the local, "a sense of place." Under the auspices of place, one's belonging, one's identity in relation to one's surroundings, is at issue; there to be negotiated, and in fact already in the process of being negotiated.

But to raise the question of trinity and place, in my experience, typically evokes a different reaction. Whether one's interlocutors are theologians or theologically invested non-specialists, the issue of immediate concern seems to be of God's limit, scale, and ultimacy. Is it not a creaturely reality, to be placed? Doesn't placed-ness coincide exactly with delimitation and contingency? This happens both in spite of, and because of, the habitual comfort with which most of us likely talk about God's "bigness," God's "height," God's maximal extension and infinite capacity, the vastness of God's scale, and other metaphors suggesting a kind of placing or spacing. The metaphor of expansiveness, when applied to divinity, usually carries with it an implied intensifier, a comparison: God is vaster than anything else and cannot be contained by anything. Thus, where bigness and expansiveness seem to add to divinity, the category of place seems—often, practically uncritically—to contract it. There is a felt danger in trying to place God, a fear that a placed deity is necessarily conditioned, and thus smaller than what is needed. Too, it seems to imply that there are areas where God's power does not extend—an exterior to God into which God cannot reach or intervene, but which press in on God from all sides. Such a deity is a thing or an artifact, even, at best a candidate for a polytheistic pantheon. It manifestly lacks the ineffability and mystery of threeness-in-oneness.

This worry is both understandable and, in the history of Christian theological reflection, well attested. But it will not do, I think, to let the explicit treatment of place drop out of trinitarian reflection, for several reasons. First, inasmuch as trinitarian theology supposes some kind of threeness attending God's very identity, notions of place will inevitably have a way of sneaking in. Triunity invites one to consider plurality and singularity, the distinction between the two, and how far that distinction extends. How could triunity fail to stir inquiries into, for example, how the three persons are arranged in relation to one another? Or whether they are all together somewhere, and whether God's one-ness consists in being located thus? Although they might seem unsophisticated once they are made explicit, such questions really cannot help but be raised, any more than one can avoid raising questions that sound temporal and tensed (in discussion of the order of processions, for example). Even if one gives an answer that disavows or explicitly refuses place—saying that the relationships between Father, Son, and Spirit are prior to place and exceed placial categories, that the three are not delimited quantities in the normal sense of limit, and that place in fact derives from *them* rather than the other way around—one has already made a theological claim about place and trinity. I believe it is best to do so systematically and explicitly.

Placing the Question

Which leads to the second reason that I believe this is a worthwhile inquiry. Two living thinkers—Jürgen Moltmann and Jean-Luc Marion—use place and triunity in structurally similar ways but to divergent ends. This is a startling pairing, to say the least. Moltmann and Marion, after all, do not form an obvious pairing as representatives of a shared theological vision. Early in his career Moltmann garnered criticism for his indebtedness to Hegel; Marion could hardly be more allergic to Hegel. Readers likely know Moltmann as a theologian of history—and in recent years, motivated by ecological concern, of space. Marion, by contrast, is a cartographer of Being, and of ontotheology. He traces its boundaries and speculates about its exterior. Moltmann is Protestant; Marion is Catholic. Trinitarian thought suffuses Moltmann's work over four decades, in both his early trilogy (*Theology of Hope*, *The Crucified God*, and *The Church in the Power of the Spirit*) and his later six-volume "Systematic Contributions" series. By contrast, Marion discusses Father, Son, and Spirit in the three volumes under consideration here (*God Without Being*, *Prolegomena to Charity*, and *Idol and Distance*), but this by no means exhausts his body of philosophical work on, for example, Descartes. It is possible to engage Marion's thought without proceeding through the entryway of trinitarian discourse. It is not possible to do so with Moltmann's.

Whence the similarity? In the broadest terms, each writer approaches certain set domains—history, space, Being—with a goal of getting a remote God back into them, or freeing God from them. Not, of course, that they believe God to be either remote or trapped, but they are concerned that incautious theology may suggest as much. Both Moltmann and Marion criticize predominant understandings of God based on problematic implications for God's relationship to a certain horizon. And for both Moltmann and Marion, place (or space) serves as a figure for horizons generally. Place—to the extent that it is made explicit at all—signals a domain already loaded with its own operations, possibilities, latencies, and conditions of presence. The proper application of trinitarian thought, therefore, will show how God relates to domains. This assumption is at work for Moltmann, and, in very different ways, for Marion.

But is this an appropriate way to envision place? Moreover, is it an appropriate end toward which to direct trinitarian thought? The present dissertation makes a case for conceiving the problem differently. Rather than mapping a triune God in relation to a set domain—even if we plan to show that God conditions the domain rather than vice versa—I propose that we ought to first inquire into how domains are designated as such. Put differently, what is location? What are we doing when we attempt to keep God "here," with us—or, alternately, to put God "out there" in some non-placed realm which signals God's utter difference? Indeed, even bracketing God, what are "here" and "there" even in an everyday sense? What is their history? What assumptions do they encode?

One need not look very far in order to turn up a starting point for placial inquiry other than the preconstituted discrete domain. Indeed, lately, one need not look very far to find alternatives to the alternatives, nor alternatives to those. As geographer Edward Relph comments, to survey all that has been written on place in the last twenty years is "like walking into the aftermath of an academic explosion. What had once been a reasonably coherent body of thought, grounded in phenomenology and mostly the concern of humanistic geographers . . . seems to have flown off in all directions." Definitions of place now range from sites of nostalgia, to nodes in social networks, to loci of desire.[1] Igniting this explosion is the sense that a dominant older model of place has expired. Among those who study the placed-ness of environments, it is increasingly implausible to suggest that place has to do mainly with simple extension and delimitation of the physical or geometric sort—where the vaster, more capacious quantity bounds and surrounds the things interior to, and less vast than, itself. One reason for the explosion is simply the shared sense that place must attach to more than simple extension. Community, identity, belonging-within, meaning making, finding, navigating . . . all of these are evoked by the phrase "a sense of place," yet none are accounted for by mere extension.

So another goal of this dissertation is to highlight the importance of asking theological versions of these same questions, and connecting them to one's doctrine of God. I will seek out placial implications of trinitarian models, as well as opportunities for rendering place questions in a trinitarian idiom. In this sense I am, admittedly, trying to rally others for a cause; I wish to persuade the reader that one's answers to questions about place matter, profoundly, for one's trinitarian thought. Terribly important are the trinitarian theologian's answers to questions such as: Is place irreducibly prior? Is place extrapolated from embodied human existence and secondarily imposed on the world by human subjects? Is it a function only of human affect? Does it emerge necessarily as soon as there is any cosmos?

---

1. Relph, "Disclosing the Ontological Depth of Place," 5.

Placing the Question

Or does place, so to speak, somehow come into being "after" God (who is in no way affected by place) yet "before" creation (which is already placed)?

These answers matter because place—in the broadest sense, the ability to point and say "that thing, there"—has everything to do with conceptual intelligibility. The link between place and intelligibility, place and epistemology, will display itself over and over again, even in the work of thinkers for whom the connection is not made explicit. Place thus refracts other inquiries central to trinitarian thought; it bends epistemology, determines the angle of ontology, and changes the course of theological method. The problems with putting God into place turn out to correlate with the problems of fixing God in conceptual thought. The need to put God in a place closely attends the need to have God available for thought.

Not surprisingly, given such an exhaustive scope, my treatment will not be definitive. It will be a first aerial sweep over a terrain that deserves to be explored on foot. (In future work, I hope to be one such explorer.) However, the fact that this dissertation represents only an initial topical survey will not stop me from offering, at the end, the roughest sketch of a constructive trinitarian theology of place. Whether it ultimately works, I really cannot say. In chapter 5 I propose it, speculate as to its strengths, flag some potential shortcomings, situate it in relation to Marion's and Moltmann's projects, and briefly indicate what would need to happen in order for it to be fully developed. I do not know but that it might pose new problems and/or contain serious contradictions that would emerge in the explication. But I raise it nevertheless, as an example of how a trinitarian model might proceed if place were thematized from the beginning.

Having described the itinerary, I ought now to set out on the route. One problem, though, stalls our departure: how am I using "place," and its related term "space"? I am arguing for a certain understanding of place (and opposing it, following Casey's convention, to space). Yet in order to lay out my rationale for doing so, I shall have to appeal to both terms whose definitions are already contested. Under such conditions, the only thing to do, it seems to me, is use "place" rather more generally and haphazardly than I think is ideal, identifying at least a working sensibility about what sorts of things place *may* include. (The constructive, theological understanding of place will come later, once I have established a need for it.) Given my interlocutors, I find it most appropriate and suggestive to use a sensibility formed by some of the same priorities and habits that have shaped Marion's and Moltmann's own projects—which also happen to be some of the same priorities that account for the placial explosion. I find this appropriate, because it requires a bit less switching between entirely different idioms and discourses. I find it suggestive because, as it turns out, the placial sensibility in question does not cohere with that advocated by Moltmann and Marion. Broadly postmodern, broadly postmetaphysical trinitarian thought diverges from postmodern, broadly postmetaphysical thought about place and space.

In the latter instance I have in mind representatives of that "certain kind of advocacy[,]," in which "the philosopher, sociologist, anthropologist, or geographer reflects in order to ally herself *with* place . . . [and] against the leveling, universalizing tendencies of modern life." Champions of "the concrete and particular" resist "the abstract and general of [the] Newtonian universe," and in so doing become "foot soldier[s] in the army of the anti-modern."[2] Specifically, in this chapter, I will be considering Marin Heidegger, Gaston Bachelard, and Yi-Fu Tuan. Not all three use Casey's or Brockelman's convention of equating "space" with the universalizing tendencies of modernity, and "place" with its remedy. Nor are the three placial advocates advocating exactly the same thing, for the same purpose, and with the same hope. Nevertheless, all three are concerned, in their placial reflection, about the experiential aspects of place which get neatly edited out when one adopts a universalizing habit. This is not the same thing as believing that environments—or indeed the cosmos—only exist as affective intra-mental phenomena. Heidegger, Bachelard, and Tuan walk this line differently, but they all walk it. In his own way, each thinker refuses to locate place exhaustively on one or the other side of a division: either in an outer preconstituted expanse of space, or in the inner self-grounding expanse of personal subjective depths. Rather, place happens, for all three, when a thinking subject seeks to organize and endow with meaning a world that she finds herself already in and part of. Environment and subject, together, enact place.

I propose this as a provisional working definition of place. I further think this makes good sense, given the two representatives of contemporary trinitarian thought I have chosen. One might expect that Moltmann, and certainly Marion, would be able to engage in—or at least endorse—aspects of this kind of advocacy, inasmuch as they too are worried about "the leveling, universalizing tendencies of modern life." Both are well versed in Heidegger, and both explicitly draw upon the same philosophical and

---

2. Brockelman, "Lost in Place?" 36–37.

phenomenological inheritance that Heidegger, Bachelard, and Tuan draw upon. In fact, these expectations prove, if not false, at least largely unmet. Moltmann and Marion may have deep sympathies with other aspects of postmodern or anti-modern critique, but do not ultimately embrace place and take a number of cues from space. A more experiential understanding of place—one endowed with themes of intelligibility and conceptual navigation—is, quite strikingly, where neither theologian can make an endorsement. Moltmann and Marion's trinitarian placings do *not* ultimately cohere with those advocated by the placial change agents. Why is this? Is there something about Christian trinitarian theology that rules out such an endorsement, even in the face of so much shared suspicion about the universalizing, reifying, and totalizing tendencies of modernity? Or is it that each theologian relies upon a certain domain having priority—and that this further commits him to an understanding of place where domains are prior? The placial sensibility I propose has the advantage of shining a light on this problem.

Domain or Perspective?

Because Heidegger and Bachelard react differently against previous understandings of place, it is appropriate to look backward at a handful of developments in placial thought.[3] One story which someone could tell about place—one story that Casey himself may be telling about place—is the story of how cosmogonies have dropped in and out of spatial and placial models. Aristotle emerges as a key transitional figure. His *Physics* are bereft of the drama of Plato's *Timaeus*, in which Necessity/Space/*khora* thrashes about, taking on "elementary sensibilia [which] cling to each other in momentary assemblages"[4] and eventually gather into regions of like things. Gone is the work of the Demiurge in bringing what order and form it can to the capacities of khora. Now place is debuted "in the cautious, finite

---

3. In the discussion that follows I have been helped invaluably by Casey, *Fate of Place*. Casey does what this section cannot: provide a comprehensive historical survey of philosophical reflection on place, beginning with ancient near eastern theogonies and concluding with such contemporary figures as Deleuze, Guattari, Tschumi, Merleau-Ponty, and Irigaray.

4. Casey, *Fate of Place*, 33–34, Timaeus 52d–53a: Receptacle "separated the most unlike kinds farthest apart from one another, and thrust the most alike closest together; whereby the different kinds *came to have different regions*, even before the ordered whole consisting of them came to be."

terms of container and limit, boundary and point."[5] Aristotle's terms also dictate a priority to place—though not in the same sort of priority held by Necessity in *Timaeus*. Quite simply, "*where* something is constitutes a basic metaphysical category . . . [It] 'takes precedence of all other things.'"[6] Apart from the entire heavens and the Unmoved Mover, everything has its own *topos idios*, special place, while belonging as well to the "common place" provided for all things by the heavens.[7] Place also, for Aristotle, includes relative position—above, below, right, left, etc.—though these are also determined by the sort of thing is that occupies that position. Thus "'[A]bove' is not anything you like, but where fire, and what is light, move. Likewise, 'below' is . . . where heavy and earth-like things move."[8]

Mostly absent in Aristotle is any process whereby undifferentiated place gathers matter or material sensibilia coalesce in localities. Here the physical world, in Casey's retelling, "takes care of itself by appearing from the start as fully formed[.] . . . [T]he only pertinent deity is an utterly stationary Mover who is (despite the appellation) eternally at rest *outside the world* and thus in effect *nowhere at all*."[9] With a fully formed world came fully formed proper places which act as containers, or vessels. The limit of a *topos idios*, and the limit of a thing's form, are in this way coextensive.[10] Both are limits, but form designates the limit of the thing, and place designates the limit of the surrounding environs.[11] Place presses in from without; it delimits and contains. No story tells the story of how place itself came to be, apart from the placed things themselves.

I offer this hastiest of sketches of Aristotle's placial innovation, because that fact helps to set up Descartes—and thereby to set up Heidegger, who understood Descartes as a transitional figure between Aristotle and Husserl.[12] (Bachelard, for his part, was sharply critical of Descartes, but calls for

5. Casey, *Fate of Place*, 50.
6. Aristotle, "Physics" 208b35 from ibid., 50.
7. Casey, *Fate of Place*, 50.
8. Aristotle, "Physics" 208b35 from ibid., 53.
9. Casey, *Fate of Place*, 56.
10. Ibid., 54.
11. Ibid.
12. I lack the space to treat Husserl here, but for the purpose of this very quick overview I think Husserl stands for phenomenology more broadly: that is, Descartes' status as transitional figure consists in his being crucial to the transition from Aristotelian physics and metaphysics to a more phenomenological approach. See Kisiel, *Genesis of Heidegger's Being and Time*, 277.

a different remediation than does Heidegger. I shall say much more about this in a moment.) At this point the picture risks becoming crowded, but such a risk is necessary. For by lining up a number of figures side by side—and of course one could easily find reason to include many, many more—we begin to see certain range of possibilities for thinking about place. Plato represents one approach; place is the result a primordial process of differentiation and gathering, which at some points requires or invites the imposition of order. Aristotle represents another approach; place is simply a given, programmed (so to speak) into the cosmic operating system. A thing's place consists in its being contained by its surroundings. Following Heidegger, let us say that Descartes (about whom I shall say more shortly) facilitates a transition to Husserl, who represents yet a third position along a trajectory, one in which a subject's lived body engages and holds sway with the surrounding life-world at which it perceives itself to be the center, with place sedimenting out of this process.[13] And of course, of those just mentioned Husserl gets closest of all these figures to Heidegger's own view (about whom I shall also say much more in a moment).

Plato, Aristotle, Descartes (whom Heidegger believed to be a transitional figure), Husserl, Heidegger. A spotty trajectory, to be sure, and one with many gaping omissions to be filled in, but a trajectory nonetheless. Without pretending to give an in-depth philosophical history, I do here note the range of possibilities for thinking about place in the philosophical tradition. But even more importantly, we see that two questions are contested: First, how (if at all) does place come about? And second, does location have to do with where things are in a fixed sense, within a cosmos viewed from no particular perspective; alternately, is location about a subject locating things in relation to him- or herself, within his or her surroundings, the world in which s/he lives?

The first question, although it need not be theological, certainly invites theological explanations, for it is not very far removed from asking where the cosmos came from, and how, and by whose (if anyone's) hand. The second question invites epistemological claims, claims about the nature of perception and the possibility of knowledge. In light of this, it is easy to appreciate why Descartes—who entertained both questions with great care—emerges as an important character in the story of place. On his

---

13. See, e.g., Husserl, *Crisis of European Sciences and Transcendental Phenomenology*, 106–7. For a summary of Husserl's thought on place, see Casey, *Fate of Place*, 216–28. On Husserl and reduction, Dermot Moran is particularly helpful: Moran, *Introduction to Phenomenology*, 124–63.

own account Descartes rejected Aristotelian philosophy early,[14] and two elements of this rejection—though they may appear disparate—help Descartes to stake out his placial options. For one, Descartes rejected Aristotle's notion that a thing's place has something to do with what it is—that hot things are located higher, that earthy things sink, and so forth. Although Descartes rejected the revived atomism of Beeckman and Gassendi, nevertheless he retained their belief that the apparent properties of bodies—including their location and motion—are best explained in terms of their constitutive parts, and not of innate tendencies of certain natures. Secondly, and more fundamentally, Descartes departed from the Aristotelian-Christian scholastic synthesis on the matter of authority. Rather than grounding his own system in the authority of senses, texts, and teachers, Descartes sought to ground his own philosophy in a more immediate certainty than that afforded by historical tradition. To this end, famously, Descartes began his philosophical system with the *cogito* argument, establishing the self as some sort of starting point for all knowledge: I am aware that I am a thinking thing, and on this point I cannot be mistaken.

This is characteristic of Descartes' method, which is to identify what the mind cannot help but conceive, and from there proceed to answer the original question which had touched off the inquiry. The existence of God, for example: the mind cannot conceive of God without conceiving of God who exists, any more than one can conceive of a triangle the measure of whose angles add up to something other than 180 degrees, or a mountain without a valley.[15] Likewise, if my mind has within it an idea of God as something that has infinite perfection, I, a finite substance, cannot have caused this idea; therefore it must have been caused by God.[16] And Descartes gives the same sort of methodological anchoring to his distinction—a crucial one, for the present purpose—between *res cogitans* and *res extensa*. In Meditation VI Descartes argues that one has a clear idea of oneself as a thinking, non-extended thing; one meanwhile also has a clear idea of one's body as an extended thing which does not think. Descartes allows this distinction tremendous influence over the rest of his system. In fact, the principle attribute of the mind is precisely to think; the principle attribute of the body is to be extended. In the case of a human person, mind and

---

14. Throughout this section on Descartes, and particularly on biographical details, I am indebted to Garber, "Descartes, René."

15. Descartes, "Meditations on First Philosophy," 170–72.

16. Ibid., 149.

Placing the Question

body are "intermingled" so closely as to allow the mind to perceive bodily sensations[17] but nonetheless this central division—between thinking thing, and extended thing—secures Descartes' place as a major character in the philosophical history of place.

Volumetric extension—envisioned in geometric terms—thus defeats Aristotle's placial vessels as the organizing spatial concept. Extension includes "whatever has length, breadth, and depth, not inquiring whether it be a real body or merely space"[18] because any such difference is one imposed by thought only. For Descartes there is no true void, no passive ontologically bereft expanse awaiting occupation by extended things. We might try to think of an entirely empty space, but this quickly proves unthinkable; even if we consciously remove every physical property in an attempt to imagine a void, whatever mental conception results still has depth and dimensionality.[19] We mentally designate as "space" whatever is filled by bodies, but in fact there is no instance of space not filled by a body; Descartes' cosmos is crowded and dense, characterized by "an insistent identification of space with *matter*, that is, with physical bodies possessing magnitude and shape."[20] Compared to extension, both space and place become derivative and relative: space, because it is at best a heuristic convention; and place, because it is entirely a function of a thing's volume, magnitude, and relative position. No more does a thing's place have anything to do with the nature of the thing—as it did for Aristotle. For Descartes, "internal place" simply denotes a thing's volume and shape, while "external place" denotes a thing's position relative to other things.[21] He can, he acknowledges, think of no reason why the cosmos should have an outer boundary, "but I would not dare to call it infinite, because I see that God is greater than the world, not in extension (for I have often said I do not think He is strictly speaking extended) but in perfection."[22]

Indeed, what of God, place, and space? Like Augustine, whom I shall consider in the next chapter, Descartes entertains the question of God's location, and finds that he must explain why God is not a materially extended

17. Ibid., 176–79.
18. Descartes, "Rules for the Direction of the Mind," 57.
19. See, e.g., Descartes' remark in *Le Monde*, chapter 4: "All those spaces that people think to be empty, and where we feel only air, are at least as full, and as full of the same matter, as those where we sense other bodies." Quoted in Casey, *Fate of Place*, 155.
20. Casey, *Fate of Place*, 152.
21. Descartes, *Principles of Philosophy*, 46.
22. Descartes, "Letter of April 15, 1649" in *Descartes: Philosophical Letters*, 250–52.

The Place of the Spirit

quantity. True to methodological form, Descartes bases his argument on the fact that we cannot imagine a God who is spatially extended. So says Descartes in reply to Henry More, who had raised the possibility. If God were spatially extended, Descartes objects, then it would be possible to imagine God as being "distinguishable into shaped and measured parts," having various parts of definite size and shape, each of which is non-identical with the others." But "[n]othing of this kind can be said about God," because of all the other things which must be true of God: necessary existence, infinite perfection, self-caused, etc.[23] So where is God—or can one not ask this question? Descartes answers by explaining, not where God is, but what God can do as a *res cogitans*. Again, his claim rests upon what we can and cannot conceive. One of the things we can conceive is that a *res cogitans*—whether God, an angel, or the human mind—"can all be at the same time in one and the same place (*locus*)."[24] Nonextended, thinking entities can be in a place, or (in God's case) even be in every place at once. This is no spatial being-in, however; "being in a place" here carries the very particular sense of being able to *act* there, to exert a power there, to make something happen there. This is precisely not the way in which extended things are in a place; for extended things in Descartes' crowded cosmos, any particular *locus* is a site for exclusivity and incompatibility.[25]

I have engaged in this all too brief discussion of Descartes, as I said earlier, for two reasons: First, one of my goals in this chapter is simply to show something of the vast range of possibilities for thinking about place. In the brief space devoted here to Plato, Aristotle, and now Descartes, certain placial variables have emerged. Earlier I indicated the difference between a domain-centric description of place (where place has to do with things and expanses, viewed from no perspective in particular) versus a view of place which emphasizes the activity of a subject in a world. I discussed, secondly, the question of the origin of space and place—a question which can invite theological inquiries inasmuch as it inquires into first causes. With Descartes, we can see that there are several additional contested questions. Under what conditions is a place a site of exclusion, that is, the sort of thing where one and only one thing can lay claim to it at one time? Descartes

23. Descartes, "Letter of February 5, 1649" from *Descartes: Philosophical Letters*, 239, quoted in Casey, *Fate of Place*, 152.

24. Descartes, "Letter of February 5, 1649" in *Descartes: Philosophical Letters*, 239. See discussion in Casey, *Fate of Place*, 151–55, as well as n. 4, p. 400.

25. God's infinity—among other things, the way in which God is everywhere—follows much this same logic.

Placing the Question

indicates that for *anything* physically extended—anything which is not a *res cogitans*—this exclusion is operative. But even Descartes—the champion of material extension—nevertheless hints that, in fact, the exercise of power over a *locus* is another way to be in that *locus:* that, in fact, it is the way appropriate to a *res cogitans*. So here is another contested issue, one not raised for the first time by Descartes but certainly flagged by his project: Is there a way to be non-materially placed—in the case of a *res cogitans* exerting power, for example—and if so, what does it involve?

All of these question return us to the overarching issue of Descartes' candidacy as a transitional figure between Aristotle and Husserl. Arguably, Aristotle represents a particularly vigorous example of the domain-focused understanding of location. For Aristotle, the "general place" of the heavens locates things, as do the individuals vessels surrounding things. They are in the places they are in, simply because of the sort of things which they are. The more contemporary, phenomenologically attuned, metaphysically suspicious placial thinkers—Heidegger and Bachelard, in the present dissertation—will contest this. They do so, as Heidegger indicates, from the far side of Descartes. For although Descartes' notion of place falls squarely in the "domain" camp, his epistemology resists such a tendency. Descartes' method rests upon the subject's experience of his or her knowledge, and the distinction between *res extensa* and *res cogitans* does, ultimately, have an anchor in the subject's perception.

Heidegger and Bachelard differ in their criticism of Descartes' strategy, and this difference has implications for Heidegger and Bachelard's understandings of place. Heidegger holds that Descartes' *cogito* ought to have been the basis, not for a coherent philosophy built upon epistemological certainty, but for more than that: a new fundamental ontology. According to Heidegger, Descartes had correctly noticed a unique characteristic of the human person—its capacity for internal, self-reflective activity—but had erred in appending that characteristic onto "thing." Heidegger, by contrast, contends that the human person *is* in a unique way. So although Heidegger praises Descartes for "providing the point of departure for modern philosophical inquiry by his discovery of the '*cogito sum*[,]'" he criticizes Descartes for overlooking the fact that a self is a "being thing" as well as a "thinking thing." Descartes investigated the *cogitare* but "leaves the '*sum*' completely undiscussed, even though it is regarded as no less primordial than the *cogito*. Heidegger seizes upon this, probing the meaning and possibility of this particular sort of being. This is the aim of Heidegger's existential analytic[26]—a project which, in the course of its exposition, unveils yet more options for thinking about place, as we shall see shortly.

For Gaston Bachelard, though, the critique of Descartes strikes a different note. Like Heidegger, he agrees with Descartes that epistemological analysis is useful, but he disagrees that such analysis should serve as the foundation of certainty for a philosophical system. The problem with eliding epistemological foundations with logical foundations, Bachelard contends, is that human knowers are not only intellects, nor are they perspective-free. Descartes therefore assumes too much when he seeks certainty based on self-reflexive inquiry, for it does not follow that whatever strikes a human intellect as epistemologically simple, immediate, or certain *must therefore be* simple, immediate, and certain relative to some objective order of things.[27] To conflate the two gives a false cover of logical certainty to all manner of subjective conventions and experiences. Bachelard sees this disingenuousness as particularly evident in the sciences, but he does not believe the remedy to consist in rooting out all bias (which would be impossible). To the contrary, for Bachelard, the genuine advantage of epistemological analysis lies in its ability to force certain questions of science. "We shall therefore ask scientists: how do you think? what are you groping after? What trials do you make, what errors? . . . Give us, above all, your vague ideas, your contradictions[.]"[28] With Bachelard's intervention, Descartes' method of critically reflexive questioning becomes—as Tiles notes—"an analysis of the mentality of a scientific community[.]"[29]

Even axioms of geometry—those favorite Cartesian examples of a particularly valuable type of certainty—become perspectival and experiential in Bachelard's hands. In chapter 4 of *The Philosophy of No*, Bachelard entertains the possibility of "eliminate[ing] all trace of mechanical, physical, or biological experience from our knowledge of space," so as to arrive at an understanding of purely geometric space. Geometric space, of course, is often understood to enjoy precisely this independent status. However, as Bachelard explains, the geometric space depends upon "linear connection," the overdetermined framing of all reality into objective things connected by relational lines.[30] Is the freighting of linear connection truly self-evident,

26. Heidegger, *Being and Time*, Division One, section 10, 71–72. See also Gelven, *Commentary on Heidegger's Being and Time*, 50–51.
27. Tiles, *Bachelard*, 33–34.
28. Bachelard, *Philosophy of No*, 11.
29. Tiles, *Bachelard*, 35.
30. Bachelard, *Philosophy of No*, 80–81.

independent, undetermined by the finite perspective of human embodied knowers? In fact, argues Bachelard, it is not, and he gives examples from mathematics and physics which resist the constraints of the (so to speak) "balls and sticks" model implied by linear connection.[31]

Likewise, the space of formal Euclidean geometry—traversed by mathematically plottable lines and containing infinite points—proves to derive from the human experience of interacting with physical objects. For Bachelard, this is to be expected and could not be otherwise. The problem is that "common intuition has been wrong in conceiving the drawing of a line with such excessive finality" and "unity of definition[.]"[32] This error has spawned other skewed, reified ways of viewing space. Even the claim that no two objects can occupy the same place at the same time, Bachelard argues, enjoys no real independence of our perspective. "There will be a strong tendency to consider this postulate as an evident axiom[,]" he warns, but in fact "this postulate is indissolubly joined to a special kind of object, an absolute solid, an impenetrable solid."[33] Indeed, this is how solids appear most easily to human beings, based on the activities of which we have keen awareness. But it does not follow, from that fact, that this is how all things independently are. As it happens, Bachelard notes, the postulate of the absolute solid is contradicted by field physics, which allows for and notices the superimposition of phenomena onto each other—"bring[ing] together different objective entities in one place, at the same moment."[34]

Alike in their ambivalent appreciation of Descartes, diverging in their proposed remediations of his project, Heidegger and Bachelard will prove to have different placial proposals. Heidegger directs attention to the underdetermined *sum* in Descartes' *cogito ergo sum*, inquiring into the being of the human subject. Bachelard, by contrast, urges modesty and—literally—a sense of perspective: epistemological analysis is useful, he suggests, not because it ground philosophical certainty or fundamental ontology, but because it reveals the vagaries and guesses and extrapolations implicit in conceptual systems. Yet by different means, both thinkers commit themselves to an analysis of how place is experienced and known—and both therefore edge away from a strictly domain-focused view of space and

---

31. Ibid., 82–84.
32. Ibid., 81.
33. Ibid., 101.
34. Ibid.

place. I shall now consider each of their placial models in turn, in greater depth.

Heidegger

In *Being and Time,* Heidegger sets out to consider Being, not in the detached mode in which one might study a particular being—the error he believes to have been made by traditional ontology—but rather as that in terms of which humanity's self-understanding is understood. "Dasein," there-being—a neologism of Heidegger's which designates a set of beings coextensive with humanity—is that being for whom Being is at issue, that creature who recursively considers its own being. Therefore it will be through an inquiry into the being of Dasein that the meaning of Being will be disclosed. But of course, this is placial from the outset. In Heidegger's "preliminary sketch" of being-in-the-world, Heidegger considers the "da," the "there," of Dasein. He contrasts Dasein's way of "being-in" with the very different sort of "being in something" that designates "the relationship . . . which two entities extended 'in' space have to each other with regard to their location in that space."[35] The latter model—the "container model," as Casey calls it—derives from Aristotle, as does the totalized "world-space" (*Weltraum*) to which Heidegger also refers: the maximally capacious holder of all less capacious holders. By contrast, Dasein inhabits the world in the manner of one who belongs there, is at home there, and cares for it.

To hide this aspect of Dasein by insisting on a world-space is to posit a fixed, cramped universe devoid of involvements—in which every locale, every punctuate and discrete site, is plotted and plottable, and every quantity is posited as exclusively present-at-hand. Placially and spatially, one finds that any available real estate has already been developed, so to speak—built up and and reified into reassuringly solid and stable things with defined positions and limits . . . such that there is no longer any "wherein," any leeway in which to move around. Absent is the room along the edge of a thing in which one might hope to observe its involvements to other things, its role in the pragmatic relationships of usefulness that comprise the everyday landscape in which human beings in fact live.[36]

Throughout *Being and Time,* and in contrast to a model of totalized world-space, Heidegger envisions a kind of "there" in which two forces have

---

35. Heidegger, *Being and Time,* 79.
36. Ibid., 134–35.

Placing the Question

acted and are active. First, there is the world's frank and prior foundness, as experienced by Dasein who finds itself thrown into the world where things are already intelligible in predetermined ways that having to do with the specific context and the community's shared practices.[37] But second, there is Dasein's activity of making things "near"—"de-distancing" things one from another so as to give them distinct directionality and significance having to do with their use, while also bringing them together into a world of other interrelated things and, further, freeing up space for them so they can be used. As I read *Being and Time*, this polarity—the pulls exercised by (in Casey's words) the "found" character of the ready-to-hand and "the founding inventiveness of Dasein"[38]—structures all discussions of Dasein's spatiality. Dasein's spatiality is what gathers and structures that very "there" where Dasein finds itself. Here we see Heidegger's characteristically phenomenological return to the things as they appear—except that, here, one of the things in question is exactly the world, with Dasein's practical concerns left intact.

To be sure, for all the focus on place in *Being and Time*—and with the centrality of concepts like world, clearing, region, there, distance, direction, nearness, etc.—it is still primarily about temporality. Heidegger holds up time, not spatiality, as being uniquely able to give coherence to Dasein's concernful activity of being-in-the-world.[39] The unifying nature of Dasein's spatiality—its ability to bring a world together—only extends so far, though, before Heidegger evidently feels compelled to explain spatiality in terms of something else. So it is that in section 70 Heidegger attempts to derive human spatiality from temporality—an attempt which he claims in a later retraction to have been "untenable."[40] Too, there is the brief section which especially vexes Casey, and which I see as being of one piece with the triumph of time: Heidegger's relegation of "regions" to "nowhere." Throughout *Being and Time*, regions—the massively public areas of involvements as they are quite simply come across by Dasein—contribute the ontic and factical reliability within Heidegger's entire placial framework. But ultimately Heidegger cannot seem to find a way to locate the regions *themselves*, at least vis-à-vis Dasein's spatiality. Beyond region, in other words, there is no

---

37. Guignon's introduction (1–41) to *The Cambridge Companion to Heidegger* was helpful to me here.
38. Casey, *Fate of Place*, 250.
39. Ibid., 244–45.
40. Heidegger, "Time and Being," 23.

The Place of the Spirit

further "where"; as he says, "'Nowhere' . . . is where any region lies." And although this nowhere "does not signify nothing," and in fact contains the "disclosedness of the world for essentially spatial Being-in,"[41] it still suggests an internal tension. Could it be that Heidegger is resistant to having unity come about through spatial means—worrying, perhaps, that such a final unity would undercut the multiplicity that Dasein's spatiality is supposed to bring together? Is this why it ultimately yields to "nowhere" in the one instance, and to temporality in the other?

In my opinion, this question continues to dog Heidegger's thoughts on spatiality, location, and place, reaching most satisfactory resolution at the end of his career. After *Being and Time*, Heidegger underwent his famous turning in which the anthropological and subjectivist bent of *Being and Time* was abandoned. No longer does Heidegger intend to focus on Dasein as uniquely constitutive or illuminative of Being. Rather, Heidegger is interested in how Being draws near to Dasein.[42] Not surprisingly, the structure of Heidegger's topology undergoes a shift as well—with nearness taking on a centrality and importance independent of Dasein's intentional making-close.

As I see it, though, certain elements of Heidegger's earlier placial thought are carried over from *Being and Time*. In Heidegger's writings of the 1930s, and again in his work after World War II, Heidegger again tries to plot (so to speak) two axes of a single gradient. First, there is the sort of there-ness that has the quality of being thrown or dispersed outwards into something, in the process encountering and (selectively) superseding limits and boundaries. Meanwhile, there is also the kind of there-ness that has to do with gathering-in, collecting, drawing near. To be sure, this is expressed differently in the 1930s than it is in the 1940s and 1950s. But there is a basic sensibility which holds true over the course of Heidegger's career, and this sensibility is very much present as early as *Being and Time*.

And what of the problem mentioned above, wherein *Being and Time* evinces Heidegger's difficulty in situating spatiality itself—trying unsuccessfully to derive it from temporality in one instance, and in another instance locating it "nowhere"? A new strategy—one that admittedly does enshrine a kind of placial violence—is laid out in *An Introduction to Metaphysics* and *The Origin of the Work of Art*, both from 1935. This, of course,

41. Heidegger, *Being and Time*, 231.
42. For a more detailed discussion of Heidegger's turning, see Moran, *Introduction to Phenomenology*, 199ff.

Placing the Question

is the period of Heidegger's writing that tends to cause commentators the most worry. In John Caputo's words, it was "the beginning of the darkest days of Heidegger's life and work." Nietzsche became more and more central, while Kierkegaard, Luther, and Aristotle dropped back. Voluntarism came to dominate Heidegger's thought to a greater degree than it had in *Being and Time*. He warned of "an encroaching nihilism, by which he meant the unwelcome effects of modernity and of modern liberal democratic institutions."[43] This suspicion of modernity comes through in force in *Introduction to Metaphysics*, in which Heidegger describes Dasein as "the site (*Stätte*) which Being requires in order to disclose itself."[44] As a site, Dasein here exhibits both the self-dispersing and the gathering-in aspects of place. Indeed, they both happen as moments in the same process, for Dasein is that creature who continually goes out of itself to stake out the place where it always already is.[45] In other words, part of Dasein's dispersive staking-out involves setting limits—which, in turn, collect and gather. "[L]imit, *peras* . . . is not something that comes to beings from outside," insists Heidegger, and "[s]till less is it a deficiency in the sense of a harmful restriction. No, the hold that governs itself . . . the having-itself . . . is the Being of beings[.]"[46] A "hold that governs itself" is in fact (according to Heidegger) properly a *polis*, a place of history. In a very real sense, limits are what gather and build worlds—a far cry from "the present-at-hand perimeter of Aristotle's surrounder."[47]

Offsetting this positive sense of limit, however, is an attendant understanding of Dasein as the self-dispersing one who surpasses—violently—"the limit of the familiar." It is the task of "[t]he violent one, the creative man" to push humanity beyond the stultifyingly uniform stability of modernity, to "compel . . . the unhappened to happen and make . . . the unseen appear."[48] Such a one "must risk the assault of non-being . . . dispersion, instability, disorder, mischief. . . . placeless confusion."[49] The two aspects of place, though in one sense inseparable, are here shown to be in conflict. The theme of conflict comes up as well in *The Origin of the Work of Art*,

43. Caputo, "Heidegger and Theology," 276–77.
44. Heidegger, *Introduction to Metaphysics*, 205.
45. Casey, *Fate of Place*, 261.
46. Heidegger, *Introduction to Metaphysics*, 62, cited in Casey, *Fate of Place*, 262 n. 94.
47. Heidegger, *Introduction to Metaphysics*, 62.
48. Ibid., 161.
49. Ibid.

19

though the violence is muted. Here it is staged somewhat differently, as a conflict between "earth" and "world," "clearing" and "concealing." Earth—that which resists comprehensibility, which self-secludes—is in a fruitful polemic struggle with world. World, in turn, designates a kind of expansive openness where truth—the openness of the Open—is revealed. The capaciousness of world in *Origin of the Work of Art* stands in some contrast to the holding, delimiting *Stätte* of *Introduction to Metaphysics*. In both, though, expansiveness—the expansiveness of a world, and/or of the creatively violent one who dares to overstep limits—arises out of a milieu which shelters and contains. And in both cases this relationship involves struggle, violent struggle in *Introduction to Metaphysics*, versus mere "striving [of] the opponents"[50] in *Origin of the Work of Art*. For one of the tasks of the work of art is to show earth for what it is: essential self-seclusion, that which "brings back and shelters everything that arises *without violation*."[51] The world sets forth the earth; the earth grounds the world in its materiality.[52]

Do we find here more candidates for the job we have yet to fill—the job of situating location itself? Heidegger's attempt to derive spatiality from temporality had failed in *Being and Time*. Meanwhile, the notion—also brought up in *Being and Time*—that regions are situated by a "nowhere" appears to have been so threatening that Heidegger backed away from it as soon as he had rather enigmatically brought it up.[53] I wonder whether Heidegger has here decided to situate spatiality as opposition—the opposition between gathering-in and going-out-beyond, between concealing and unconcealing, between delimiting and surpassing, between capaciousness and closeness. For in a way we return to the same problem we returned to before: what sort of a "there" can contain the two reagents which together to yield there-ness, yield presence? Certainly not a totalized, present-at-hand expanse. One sensible answer is that the irreducible opposition is what situates the two. At the very least, such a strategy protects against any lurking totality in which earth and world (for example) show up.

But that is not the only answer given by Heidegger in the 1930s. For here, the Open also situates, in a non-totalizing fashion. And in the 1950s and 1960s, when Heidegger returns again to place, this is the line he

50. Heidegger, "Origin of the Work of Art," 55.
51. Ibid., 42.
52. Casey, *Fate of Place*, 266.
53. This is Casey's interpretation in his chapter on Heidegger, "Proceeding to Place by Indirection: Heidegger," 243–82.

decides to develop. Softened, at least, is the 1930's notion that place sediments out of a primordial opposition. Too, since Heidegger has abandoned the anthropological focus of *Being and Time*, he is not restricted to defining nearness as Dasein's giving directionality to equipment within an everyday context. Consequently it is the Open which holds promise as some sort of milieu for place, but as Casey points out, its biggest advantage is also its disadvantage. Indeed, the Open allows the burden of clearing not to fall entirely upon Dasein's shoulders, but for this very reason it threatens to become yet another version of totalized infinite space.[54]

To address this threat, the later Heidegger detotalizes the Open by issuing an across-the-board gerundizing. "Nearing," "gathering," and "thinging" become central, and aligned.[55] Even more so than in *Being and Time*, Heidegger is here allergic to thinking of things as preconstituted entities in any sense. Rather, "thinging" indicates the dynamic activity of serving as a gathering-place in which the fourfold of earth and sky, divinities and mortals is concentrated and condensed. Crucially, though, the fourfold are also gerundized. They are "world-regions"[56] whose activity is "regioning"—i.e., serving as the regions in which thinging takes place.[57] We thus have here a reciprocal sort of placing where the thing is the seat where regions are gathered, even as the thing is also regioned by the fourfold. A thing is, so to speak, *here*, but it is also *a here* for the fourfold. Such reciprocity resists any tendency of the Open to become a stable, totalized, fully realized expanse—all without relying on primordial struggle bordering on violence. Instead, the Open retains its intended sense of detotalized possibility, through the coinherence of gathering and clearing implicit in any "here" or "there."

In sum, then, Heidegger shows one possible way of thematizing place in such a way that accounts for both subjective experience and the givenness of the world. The ways in which he does this change over the course of his career. His evaluation of Descartes, and his search for formal structures of place, show Heidegger's ontological focus. This is not the focus of Gaston Bachelard, and one could guess as much from Bachelard's own criticism of Descartes. For Bachelard, the payoff of existential analysis is simply the light it sheds upon experience. One need not, and ought not, ask this to ground a fundamental ontology or philosophical system. Nevertheless, one

---

54. Casey, *Fate of Place*, 280.
55. Heidegger, "Thing," 165.
56. Heidegger, "Nature of Language," 104ff. Also cited by Casey, *Fate of Place*, 281.
57. Heidegger, "Nature of Language," 103.

can say of Bachelard, too, that his understanding of place admits both subjective experience and the givenness of the world. One may see this most clearly in the traits he attributes to the home in his work *The Poetics of Space*. To that work I now turn.

Bachelard's Poetics of Space

Where Heidegger sought a more formal structure of place, Bachelard is primarily interested in observing how place operates. And where Heidegger had traditional metaphysics in the crosshairs throughout his career, Bachelard's polemical partners are more varied and veiled. At the end of *The Poetics of Space* Bachelard takes on metaphysics explicitly, and he reserves some critical remarks for philosophy more generally. Too, we earlier examined how Bachelard criticizes the presumed objectivity of science in *The Philosophy of No*. In *Poetics of Space* all of these criticisms are rehearsed, and we also see Bachelard's friendly rivalry with psychoanalysis. In dialogue with all of these discourses, Bachelard—differently, though no less than, Heidegger—expounds upon the experiential, concernful aspects of location.

Indeed, as a way of proceeding toward the "working placial sensibility" which is the goal of this chapter, I shall at this point float a hypothesis: In Bachelard's *Poetics of Space,* as in Heidegger's placial reflections throughout his career, we see a similar clustering of concepts and images. Place, it is thought, has to do at once with closing-in-on and opening-out-to, with concealing and unconcealing, with delimiting and going-out-beyond, with drawing-near and surpassing. I have hunted for an apt metaphor to describe the relationship between these clusters. In one sense they are rather like a polarity, mutually implying each other; in another they are like chemical reagents, since place is produced from the reaction between the two. Alternately, they are like two axes of a grid along which a function is plotted—the function being place itself. All of these metaphors, though, threaten to obscure one of the most important features of the placial sensibility I have been uncovering, which is this: the two components of place are not themselves found within some lurking prior "where," some less-reducible expanse, some overarching totality, within which they show up. There is no place other than that place yielded by the coinherence of closing and opening, nearness and expansiveness, sheltering and ekstasis.

Placing the Question

For Bachelard, this pertains first and foremost to the psyche—the place with which Bachelard is concerned. Throughout *The Poetics of Space*, Bachelard insists that the human psyche has its own unique sort of placial parameters, its own sort of insideness—neither empty nor geometric nor physical.[58] The psyche, for Bachelard, is the "where" appropriate to a poetic image, which flashes across the psyche's surface and reverberates in its depths. Even so, the psyche does not end up functioning as the irreducible place which underlies all opening and closing. To the contrary, the unique interiority and directionality of the psyche only ever operates in relationship to physical spaces—in particular, the intimate physical localities of everyday life. Likewise, these intimate localities are only experienced through their complex way in which they, in all their multiplicity, open onto and enclose the psyche. Thus, the placiality appropriate to each realm depends upon a dynamic sort of mutual situating. There are at least two moments here: one in which the subject's familiar environs are inhabited and experienced, and another in which the psyche creatively places the images that bubble up within it as a consequence of this sort of inhabitation. It is not unlike the later Heidegger; we are talking here about a locale which serves as the place for the very environs which also place it.

The first house is an intimate locality to which Bachelard devotes significant attention. At great length he considers childhood homes, a child's experience of his or her home, and images of childhood homes in the work of such poets as Rilke and Baudelaire. Bachelard prowls through chests and wardrobes (chapter 3), corners (chapter 6), and other of the semi-enclosed spaces that make up a house as experienced by a child. The meditations read a bit like daydreams; in fact, invoking and evoking the daydream is one of Bachelard's points. The preference for daydream over dream has twofold significance. First, it contains, in a single activity, the two aforementioned moments: the experience of inhabiting an environment which one has simply come across and the experience of placing that environment through a kind of constructive, inventive action. Second, the category of "daydream" signals that Bachelard—like Heidegger—sees himself to be about the business of dressing down totalizing discourses.

Specifically, Bachelard is conscious that he is inserting the daydream into the privileged spot where psychoanalysis had placed the dream. Acknowledging the importance of dream interpretation in psychoanalysis, Bachelard notes that such interpretation "requires an all-inclusive

---

58. Casey, *Fate of Place*, 288.

symbolism to determine its interpretations"[59] To the question, "What do stairs mean in dreams?" psychoanalysis can give a descriptive answer that links a certain thing—stairs—with a certain meaning. The manner of the linking is standardized and uniform: "stairs" correlates with its proper interpretation in the same way that "thunderstorm" correlates with its proper interpretation.

But in the daydream, which is placed both by the psyche and by the physical setting, meaning is not nearly so uniform. "[T]he poetic daydream, which creates symbols, confers upon our intimate moments an activity that is poly-symbolic,"[60] yet psychoanalysis exactly fails to account for this poly-symbolism. Psychoanalysis cannot trace, in all their "longitudinal detail,"[61] the lines and surfaces of the particular staircase in familiar and beloved home. Nor can it account for the relationship between the creaking floorboards, secret hiding places, and polished tabletops of one's home, and the complex symbolics that arise when this "eulogized space"[62] finally appears on the surface of the psyche having reverberated in its depths. Nor, finally, can psychoanalysis give an account of how these intimate, idiosyncratic spaces yield poetic images which in turn resonate in the psyches of others—even those unfamiliar with the poet's first house.

Suggestion rather than description. Causality offset by reverberation. A preference for polysymbolism and ambiguity over static symbolic interpretations. A distaste for totalizing discourses, and criticism of "geometrists." A sort of place (the psyche) which refuses to behave in the way that Euclidean space behaves. And an understanding of symbolic meaning which likewise refuses to behave in a uniform, static, abstract or punctuate manner. All of these are familiar themes, even though Bachelard deploys them to different ends than did Heidegger. When Bachelard offers a counterconstruction—calling the childhood home "a cosmos in every sense of the word,"[63] and scolding those philosophers who "know the universe before they know the house."[64]—he does so in ways that fly in the face of plottable, uniform spaces and places. The house-world, though in possession

59. Bachelard, *Poetics of Space*, 26.
60. Ibid.
61. Ibid.
62. Ibid., xxxv.
63. Ibid., 4.
64. Ibid., 5.

Placing the Question

of a kind of "objectivity," still "live[s] humanly."[65] It "grows and spreads,"[66] it defends its inhabitants against winter chill and thunderstorm. It resists fixity; "[t]he space we love is unwilling to remain permanently enclosed." Precisely as an archetypal image, the house "deploys and appears to move elsewhere without difficulty; into other times, and on different planes of dream and memory."[67] Bachelard's approach here coheres with his approach in *Philosophy of No*: he exposes assumptions which have been falsely given a cover of objectivity and universality, through a two-pronged attack. First, he shows them to be drawn from lived human experience after all. Second, he gives counterexamples—phenomena which do not behave according to the conventions passing themselves off as "objective" descriptions.

Take, for example, Bachelard's meditation upon "Miniature" in chapter 7. Here Bachelard is interested in the capacity of the imagination to open up vast miniature worlds inside tiny nuclei of space (such as an apple, a pocket of air inside a pane of glass, a flower. Even in those spaces that strike the subject as tiny, vast and expansive worlds open up and out. Although "[p]sychologists—and more especially philosophers—pay little attention to [this] play of miniature,"[68] Bachelard argues, it is just this sort of analysis which delivers what logic cannot. "One must go beyond logic," he continues, "in order to experience what is large in what is small."[69] Logic belongs to the "mind that observes," and the final result of observation is invariably "a diagram that summarizes acquired learning."[70] But the poetic imagination cannot operate according to such strictures. The "mind that imagines" follows the "opposite path," multiplying images rather than distilling them—by, for example, using images from one scale (the scale of a room or cosmos) to describe things of another scale (the interior of a flower). In so doing, the imagination invests environs with value, making possible the reverie of "relax[ing] . . . in a small space."[71]

But how does this constitute a redemption of geometrical contradiction? Or indeed, how is it—as Bachelard will say shortly thereafter—a "liberation"[72]? As I understand *The Poetics of Space*, the redeeming, liberat-

65. Ibid., 48.
66. Ibid., 51.
67. Ibid., 53.
68. Ibid., 148.
69. Ibid., 150.
70. Ibid., 151–52.
71. Ibid., 162.
72. Ibid., 154–55.

ing aspects issue from their disruption of "all obligations of dimensions."[73] There is a theme of freedom in *Poetics of Space,* the freedom of one who is free to daydream, as well as the freedom of one released from restrictive confines. Here the imagination clears psychic space by being *freed from* the more restrictive aspects of both physical space and of the mind that observes. The psyche is freed, in other words, to inhabit the placial parameters appropriate to it, where reverberation takes precedence over causality and vastness and miniature coinhere.

I have not said much about vastness until this point, but I think it appropriate to introduce it here. As I read him, Bachelard means for us to connect the coinherence of vastness and smallness with the coinherence of enclosure and freedom offered by intimate spaces. Indeed, vastness is first experienced in the "enlarging gaze of a child"[74] exploring her or his first cosmos, the home. Vastness thus operates according to the same placial parameters as miniature. The experience of a world opening out expansively beyond oneself—giving one freedom in which to move around—is, paradoxically, "most active in the realm of intimate space."[75] As with a miniature world, a vast world is an instance of capaciousness *within* enclosure, where each depends on and implies the other. Bachelard's point, if I understand him correctly, is that these sorts of places are the ones in which our most important moments are spent—the overreaching claims of geometry notwithstanding. The placiality he has been describing is the sort of placiality appropriate to imagination, poetry, reverie . . . indeed, to our very psyches themselves, in which vastness and enclosure, freedom and intimacy *also* coinhere.

Naturally, these aforementioned commitments ultimately press Bachelard into an explicit consideration of inside and outside, and—even more crucially—of limit. Of the spatial pair of "outside" and "inside," Bachelard asserts that the "obvious geometry" of these words "blinds us as soon as we bring it into play in metaphorical domains."[76] Diagramming, rendering, "draw[ing] circles that overlap or exclude" . . . geometric proclivities such as these cannot help but obscure the intimacy of insideness, the openness of outsideness, and the relationship between the two. Such a geometry "has the sharpness of the dialectics of *yes* and *no,* which decides everything"

73. Ibid.
74. Ibid., 155.
75. Ibid., 192.
76. Ibid., 211.

and which is metaphysically expressed. "Philosophers," he continues, "when confronted with outside and inside, think in terms of being and non-being." This reduction results in a "profound metaphysics . . . rooted in an implicit geometry which—whether we will or no—confers spatiality upon thought."[77] Open and closed thus become concepts within a system, "metaphors that he [the philosopher] attaches to everything[.]"[78] Here and there become "promoted to the rank of an absolutism according to which these unfortunate adverbs of place are endowed with unsupervised powers of ontological determination."[79] Bachelard goes so far as to call this a "geometrical cancerization of the linguistic tissue of contemporary philosophy."

Lest we doubt who he has in mind, Bachelard also takes issue with the *être-là*, being-there. Heidegger—and this critique should not surprise us, given the substantial difference in how each thinker views Descartes—errs, according to Bachelard, by trying to make the intimate spaces of daily life into an ontology. For Bachelard, intimate space need not, and ought not, be linked to ontology; surely (one imagines him imploring) it is enough simply to allow intimate space to be intimate space. For, as he has said all along, this sort of space—poetic, intimate, psychic space—has its *own* operations appropriate to it. It has its own depths and surface. It need not be conjoined to Being or to causality or volumetric extension. When linked, the asymmetry of *être* and *là*, of *da* and *Sein*, threatens to distort one or the other, to define one in terms of the other. "What is the main stress," he asks, "in *being-there*: on *being*, or on *there*?" Regardless of the answer, the result can only "the dogmatization of philosophemes as soon as they are expressed."[80] Inside and outside thus risk degenerating into a kind of "first myth."[81] By contrast, when inside and outside are freed from such metaphysical responsibilities, the tendency to oppose the two also relaxes. A good thing, for it turns out such primordial opposition is ill suited for describing the spaces we inhabit. He invites us to consider, as an example, a room in a home. Although it is "outside" us, and we are "inside" it, we do not in fact experience a sharp limit where we leave off and the room begins.

---

77. Ibid., 211–12.
78. Ibid., 212.
79. Ibid.
80. Ibid., 213.
81. Ibid., 212. Bachelard is quoting Jean Hyppolite's spoken commentary on the *Verneinung* of Freud, and cites *La Psychoanalyse* No. 1, 1956, p. 35.

Rather, "[t]o inhabit such a room is for *it to be in us*, and for us to be in an entire house and world *through it*."[82]

And yet, this is not altogether dissimilar from Heidegger's assertion in "Building, Dwelling, Thinking." For Heidegger writes: "I am never here only, as this encapsulated body; rather I am *there*, that is, I already pervade the room[.]"[83] Of course, *Poetics of Space* was originally published in 1958, and thus was roughly contemporary with Heidegger's later writings discussed in the preceding section. I mention Heidegger's quotation not to suggest that there is no substantial disagreement between Heidegger and Bachelard. There is, on the contrary, a profound disagreement: whether or not one should be concerned with the capacity of place to disclose something about Being. For Heidegger, this is the whole point. For Bachelard, it amounts to an alarmingly inappropriate use of place. But for the present purpose—which has, after all, to do more with place than with ontology—we ought not overlook the profound agreement between the two thinkers. Indeed, the substance of the disagreement reveals how much the two share; Bachelard's criticisms reveal that he—with Heidegger—cannot abide an overly geometrized, totalized definition of place.

Yi-Fu Tuan

Finally, and yet further along this (very broadly defined) trajectory, we turn at last to geographer Yi-Fu Tuan's 1974 books *Topophilia* (1974) and *Space and Place: The Perspective of Experience* (1977). As I indicated (perhaps too cryptically) in the introduction, Tuan is a less obvious choice to introduce in this dissertation. It is clear that Tuan is conversant with continental philosophy—though his writing style is more evocative than explicitly polemical, or even overtly philosophical—but ultimately Tuan is a humanistic geographer, not a philosopher. Within the field of geography, "humanistic" denotes one of the two main reactions, instigated in the 20th century, against quantitative geography. (The other was Marxist geography.) Yi-Fu Tuan was and is one of the architects of this sub-field. As such, he characteristically engages questions about human valuing of built environments, as evidenced in art, ritual, literature, and the practices of everyday life. "Topophilia" refers, for Tuan, to "the affective bond between people and

---

82. Bachelard, *Poetics of Space*, 223.
83. Heidegger, "Building, Dwelling, Thinking," 157.

place or setting[,]"[84] and inquiry into topophilia includes question about ideals, economics, language, and metaphor. Largely following Tuan's lead, humanistic geography has characteristically emphasized "place," understood broadly as "sense of place"—and in so doing situated itself as one of the predominant discourses in the "certain kind of advocacy" mentioned by Brockelman. Somewhat surprisingly, though, Tuan does not oppose space to place, nor does "space" denote "uniform, geometric, volumetric space." Rather, for Tuan, both "space" and "place" require and yield each other; space is an extrapolation from place, and place requires an incipient assumption about space. The dynamic between the two is irreducible. Neither place nor space settles into a fully realized, fully present totality.

This is the relationship Tuan explores in his second, very influential monograph, *Space and Place: the Perspective of Experience*. Tuan, like Bachelard, is content to suggest when it would be too heavy handed to describe. *Space and Place*—much like *The Poetics of Space*—contains many discrete meditations on various kinds of places and spaces as they are discovered and experienced in human life. For Tuan, the relationship of place and space is the relationship between—and the coinherence of—freedom and security, which finds locative expression as expansiveness and enclosure. "Place," he explains, "is security, space is freedom."[85] Indeed, the sense of being free "implies space; it means having the power and enough room in which to act."[86] Space is a visit to the seashore after being confined in a cramped, walled city—to cite the example Tuan gives from Paul Tillich's childhood.[87] Place, by contrast, is the family home of Bachelard's *Poetics of Space*, intimately known by its inhabitants. Space is "more abstract," to the point that a very large space—"our country if it is very large"—cannot be known, but only known about.[88] Place, inasmuch as it is security, is also "concretion of value."[89] In the structuring of worlds, humans attach value to the elements of their lives. Some of these values—like security—attach not to objects that can be carried around, but to the environments which humans inhabit. A place so imbued with value therefore functions "like a cherished object, one which signifies all sorts of things to its handler."[90]

84. Tuan, *Topophilia*, 4.
85. Tuan, *Space and Place*, 3.
86. Ibid., 52.
87. Ibid., 3–4.
88. Ibid., 6.
89. Ibid., 12.
90. Ibid.

Place "satisfies something other than science."[91] By way of illustration, Tuan quotes physicist Niels Bohr's amazement at "'how this castle changes as soon as one imagines that Hamlet lived here . . . As scientists we believe that a castle consists only of stones. . . . None of this should be changed by the fact that Hamlet lived here, and yet it is changed completely.'"[92]

In a way this recalls the later Heidegger—with his condensed "thinging" and "regioning"—as well as that of Bachelard, with his talk of values accreting to places. Tuan attends especially to the factors that give value to places—their temperature, the pain or comfort they bring us, the physical protection they offer.[93] Indeed, here his imagery is striking in its depiction of portability and tangibility; such value is so condensed in a place, the value itself becomes an object in the palms of a reverent handler. Of course, freedom—the freedom of having enough of an arena in which to move and act—is another such value. It, too, attaches to the locative structure . . . but of space, not place. Is space then, for Tuan, a simply subset of place? Not exactly. For space involves a kind of extrapolating beyond oneself, beyond one's own experience, that place does not require. Which is not to say experiential aspects are ruled out—in order to experience environs as a space, one needs to experience them as spacious. But space, which is by definition vast, "is not directly perceived." There is an excessive quality to vastness, a bringing out of familiarity into the beyond. An experience of space, of vastness, thus comes about through a kind of mental multiplication of impressions[94] which are then organized in conformity with external points of reference.[95] For space, orientability is at issue; one is concerned about one's capacity to navigate within horizons that open out onto the unfamiliar, in a way that one is not in a place.

All of this is not to imply, however, that place and space are discrete opposites—let alone posit a uniform geometric expanse. For Tuan as for our other two conversation partners, vastness and enclosure both yield and depend on each other. Given Tuan's experiential and humanistic focus, the mechanism for such reciprocity should come as no surprise: it is precisely the capacity for humans to take sensory evidence and extrapolate beyond it. An experience of vastness—of space, and hence of freedom—depends

---

91. Ibid.
92. Ibid., 4.
93. See the whole of Tuan's chapter 2, "Experiential Perspectives."
94. Tuan, *Space and Place*, 16.
95. Ibid., 36–37.

Placing the Question

on the mental extrapolation of condensed, value-laden places. We know, Tuan seems to suggest, that such extrapolations introduce a sense of open uncertainty; for this reason, navigability and orientability become pressing matters when one is locating oneself in space.[96] But space also involves a kind of mental extrapolation and mythologizing.

"Mythical space," for Tuan, is extrapolated, abstracted, postulated based on the known. Tuan delineates two types: First, there is that "fuzzy area of defective knowledge surrounding the empirically known" which "frames pragmatic space."[97] By way of example: as I write this, I have a dim awareness of the bookshelf behind me, the hallway at the end of which sits my office, and the nearby thoroughfare on which I will drive to get home. But this mythical space extends further, if one is willing to abide ever-greater haziness; it might include, "successively, the rest of the house, city streets and landmarks, and other cities scattered over the broad face of the nation, all of which are roughly ordered in a compass grid," with myself at the center.[98] If one could compare the contents of my dim awareness with the actual landscapes, one would find many factual errors. The importance of mythical space, however, lies not in its being an accurate representation of all that is out there, such that one could go and verify it. Rather, such "tacit knowledge is necessary to [one's] sense of being at home and oriented in a small arena of activity."[99] I rely upon such "fuzzy ambience" to provide context and confidence in what I do know, as I carry on my practical involvements.[100]

Mythical space is constructed as well by cultural groups, Tuan points out, citing societies that "require legendary islands to fill out their space," or contemporary Western urban-dwellers who know their own neighborhood, are ignorant of the area occupied by a neighboring group, yet "share a common store of hazy knowledge (myths) concerning a far larger field—the region or nation—in which their own local areas are embedded."[101] This tendency is, Tuan muses, a possible human universal: the way in which humans do not limit their construction of place and space only to the narrow sphere of human life which directly concerns them, but instead seem

96. Ibid., 37.
97. Ibid., 86.
98. Ibid.
99. Ibid., 87.
100. Ibid., 86–87.
101. Ibid., 88.

to require that "[t]he small worlds of direct experience [be] ... fringed with much broader fields known indirectly through symbolic means."[102]

There is also, for Tuan, a second kind of mythical space—the space of cosmologies, of systems, of totalities. These are "better articulated and more consciously held than mythical space of the first kind."[103] Cosmologies reflect a more universal human need for a sense of order. But compared to the first sort of mythical space, cosmologies are more elaborate codified systems that make claims about the place of nature, humanity, and society. And this move hints at another conviction which all three placial thinkers may share: a formally similar understanding that systematically plotted space is in fact a secondary abstraction of space as it is experienced. Tuan makes this observation is made so irenically that it really cannot register as an anti-modern critique. He is not here laying a foundation for a subsequent criticism of western metaphysics, modernity, or totalizing spaces. Tuan is not Heidegger, nor is he Ed Casey. The two examples of cosmological schemata which Tuan gives are cosmologies wherein the human body is a microcosm of the universe, and cosmologies wherein the human being is at the center of a cosmic frame,[104] neither of which scans as uniquely modern. It is quite possible—not ruled out, not straightforwardly affirmed—that Tuan believes one can plot expanses objectively and scientifically. Nevertheless, for Tuan, this process still comes secondary to the "structuring of worlds": the experiential aspect of living in, and making sense of, surroundings experienced as given. On this point he is entirely consistent with Heidegger and Bachelard.

Thus mythical space ultimately yields "spatial lore." "Spatial lore" names those accretions of value that attach to space. Note the contrast: the value that attaches to place (with its connotations of familiarity and security) behaves like a cherished object. The value that attaches to space, by contrast, behaves like a cultural story. It would be an example of spatial lore, for example, to hold forth the center as the place of primary importance, or link "right" with "limit" and 'left' with "unlimited" (as in the spatial lore of the Pythagoreans).[105] Tuan's point, if I understand him correctly, is that the relationship between place and space is rather like the relationship between cherished objects and stories. Experientially, affectively, each

102. Ibid.
103. Ibid.
104. Ibid.
105. Ibid., 98.

Placing the Question

requires the other for the very accretion of value on which it relies. Spatial lore extrapolates from cherished places, just as mythologies extrapolate from cherished objects. Conversely, cherished places condense the value conferred by spatial lore, just as cherished objects condense the value conferred by shared cultural stories. In turn, these two activities—expanding, extrapolative space-making and enfolding, tactile place-making—enact human freedom and security.

By now this approach will likely strike the reader as familiar. Indeed, it is the most salient feature of the placial sensibility I have been trying to promote here: a preference for an active, reciprocal, multiplying, irreducible understanding of place and space. But this is somewhat of an interesting wrinkle, for of course Yi-Fu Tuan is a structuralist. He is a structuralist explicitly, in deliberate contradiction of (and reserving harsh criticism for) the trends towards post-structuralism and deconstruction. In one of the many "Dear Colleague" letters he continues to self-publish in his retirement, Tuan explains his preference for structuralism and the manner in which he applies it. Structuralism, he explains, teaches that there are certain "fundamental operations of thought" which cause all people to "organize reality in opposed pairs—for instance, white/black, up/down." Further, because of a "near universal recognition of the importance of the sun," most human societies have created a structural framework wherein they "see themselves living at the center of opposed pairs of north and south, east and west," and then "attribute value to these points of reference such that, for instance, north is winter and black, south is summer and red, east is spring and green, west is autumn and white." Tuan closes by affirming that he hopes his students (and, presumably, readers) will hear in his words both "the recognition of difference" and "the recognition of human commonality." Cultures are idiosyncratic and particular, making wildly different artifacts and systems out of certain basic human habits of structuring the world.[106]

Is this not, though, simply another data point suggesting a close connection between placial models and epistemology? If Tuan is correct that there are universal human ways of generating concepts and language, then it stands to reason that certain locations would be endowed with common symbolic and conceptual importance. Likewise, if—as Tuan suggests—all human beings navigate space and place in certain predetermined ways simply by virtue of being human, and the generation of concepts springs

---

106. Tuan, "Dear Colleague."

(at least in part) from one's navigation of one's environment, then it follows that conceptual and linguistic representation will bear this out. My point here is not to come down for or against Tuan, but rather to show the close connection between theories of place and space and understandings of conceptual representation and navigation. I suggest this connection only becomes more important when exploring the ways in which placial models and trinitarian models imply and limit each other. As we shall see in the next chapter, fourth century trinitarian thought interweaves place, space, and knowledge of God—in ways not always thematized or treated systematically, but apparent nonetheless, and theologically significant.

Now that we have identified a working sensibility of place, we are in a better position to flag those instances where trinitarian theology is placed. Place, I have been suggesting, has ultimately to do with how human knowers endow the found world with meaning, directionality, and navigability. The stated aims of this chapter were, first, to identify some contested issues in theories of place and space and, second, to settle upon working sensibility of place that will carry the dissertation to the point of my being able to argue constructively for a more theological, trinitarian understanding of place. To this end I chose interlocutors based on their currency, the degree to which they thematize place and space, and the facility with which they can be brought into dialogue with the contemporary trinitarian theologians I shall consider later. In closing, though, I do not wish to gloss over the differences between them. This chapter placed a lot of placial options on the table. Although the general and provisional definition of place will help identify placially significant theological moves—especially important when the theologian in question does not treat place systematically—I do not offer it in order to harmonize the placial options, nor to resolve the points of contention. Navigation and meaning making in a somewhat comprehensible world which one did not invent, but in which one moves with some degree of freedom—place will involve at least this.

2

Patristic Precedents

Enter the Trinity

IN THE PREVIOUS CHAPTER I DISCUSSED SEVERAL CONTESTED QUESTIONS in placial reflection, among them: What (if anything) causes place? Is place primarily a feature of preconstituted expanses, or of subjective experience and intellection, or of both? Do certain places signify things across cultures? And finally, what accounts for the seeming association between placial analysis and epistemological analysis? I also proposed a working definition of place—or better, placial sensibility—on which to base my later constructive proposal. Taking cues from Bachelard, Heidegger, and Tuan, I suggested that place, generally speaking, is best understood as having to do with both subjective experience and the given-ness of the world. Each of the three thinkers just mentioned parse this differently, but each uphold it; and moreover, this understanding of place draws on some of the same philosophical currents which influence Moltmann and Marion.

In this chapter I shall leap backward in time to the fourth century, the time during which many of the foundations of Christian trinitarian thought were laid down. For this is not just a dissertation on place, but on place and trinity. When one takes a placial eye to trinitarian theology, one notices placial language and concepts were a part of trinitarian discourse from the beginning—and, further, that their presence tends to indicate questions about how human beings can have knowledge of God.

I shall then all too briefly discuss four trinitarian models—two ancient, and two contemporary—as evidence for an affirmative answer to this question. I chose these particular theologians because they help me to tell a particular story, one in which encountering the Logos—perceiving it, receiving it, having it show up within some kind of field or horizon or experience—means very different things depending on one's assumptions about place. So, too, with the Spirit. How one understands the Spirit's work to be "here" in creation, depends in no small way upon what one understands by "here." These placial assumptions, I suggest, invariably become formalized in a theologian's understanding of the trinity.

Laying the problem out in this fashion goes a long way toward suggesting which sorts of passages are most attention worthy for the present project. What I am looking for is some kind of consonance between how an author positions the three persons vis-à-vis each other, and how that same author understands place more generally. Sometimes the influence will run more in one direction—a theologian's assumptions about place dictating how the three persons may be conceptually arranged—and sometimes it will run in the opposite direction. Most often, I think, we see a dual influence, a sympathy between what triunity is supposed to accomplish and how place and place are supposed to work. And, of course, there are also important points of dissimilarity as well, which I shall try to note: the stops, the qualifications, the reserve that each author uses to keep God God and creation created.

With that, let us turn to the focus of the present chapter. Here I shall consider a few examples of the placial elements of fourth century trinitarian thought, and how they intersect with theories of knowledge on the one hand and pneumatology on the other. These are offered as examples only, albeit ones particularly fruitful for the constructive project I will begin to sketch in chapter five. I regret that these will need to be offered as examples only—rather than a more systematic treatment of patristic notions of place—but the scope of my argument requires it. I shall discuss four church fathers (Basil of Caesarea, Gregory Nazianzen, Gregory of Nyssa, and Augustine) and the three conceptual angles (pneumatology, place, and theory of knowledge); and one could write an entire dissertation by taking any name from the first grouping and pairing it with any theme from the second. That said, I have not chosen my interlocutors haphazardly. Pneumatology, triunity, and the possibility for knowledge of God—all of these occupy Christian theological reflection to a profound degree in the fourth and early fifth centuries, and happily that has been covered by abler interpreters than I.[1] What I shall attempt to contribute, though, is attention to

---

1. To name but one example, Jaroslav Pelikan's Gifford lectures treat exactly this

how those theological concerns draw upon, refuse, qualify, and illuminate place—or better, placial language and metaphors; since place itself is not categorized in the way which I will ultimately advocate for.

One more preliminary word on my choice of interlocutors. Pitting Augustine's trinitarian thought against that of the Cappadocian fathers has become a well-established and well-pedigreed theological move. Whereas the Basil and the Gregories defined the three divine persons through their relationships to each other, the argument goes, Augustine affixed the trinity to a single and static divine essence. This is believed to account for the persistent tendency in the West to stick with a metaphysic of substance, a universe of fixed and self-enclosed things only incidentally related to all the other fixed and self-enclosed things. God, on this view, winds up as the very thingiest of things—so fixed as to be unchanging, so unconditioned as to need nothing, never changing, never qualified. In order to resolve this unhappy state of affairs, the West would do well (according to this particular critique) to retrieve some theological resources from the East, which has consistently outperformed the West in its ability to find a place for relation and alterity. In particular, a more Cappadocian trinitarian theology would present God in terms of dynamic relation rather than fixed essence. Versions of this criticism have been offered by, among others, Karl Rahner, Catherine Mowry LaCugna, John Zizioulas and Colin Gunton. Recent years have seen a reaction against this tendency, with Lewis Ayres, Michel Rene Barnes, and John Cavadini urging caution against reductive or anachronistic readings of Augustine—readings, for example, that portray Augustine as a Neo-Platonist with only the thinnest of Christian veneers; or, conversely, readings that portray Augustine as fundamentally an exegete of a proto-modern subjectivity.[2]

I do not intend to engage this dispute head-on, but I cannot manage to sidestep it entirely. Within the very narrow confines I have specified—that is, the placial aspects of these thinkers' trinitarian models and theological epistemology—I do detect a fundamental similarity. Basil, Nyssen, Nazianzen, and Augustine all sense a similar danger when it comes to placing the trinity: the danger that human knowledge may presume to mark and measure God. (This is, to put it mildly, a worry shared by at least one of the contemporary theologians we shall consider, Jean-Luc Marion.) There may well be a difference in emphasis, on this point, between a generally

---

nexus of themes in Cappadocian theology. Pelikan, *Christianity and Classical Culture*.

2. Cavadini, "Darkest Enigma," 119–32.

Cappadocian expression of this worry and Augustine's expression. For the Cappadocians, delimiting something conceptually typically involves a movement around the boundary of the thing—a delimitation, a marking of a perimeter. This holds when they warn against making God into something circumscribed (*perigrapton*). I see it evoked as well by *epinoia*, the abstracted means of apprehending the hidden things which are true of God but which nonetheless do not presume to pick out the divine nature. For Augustine, generally, knowledge about God is refracted onto finite intellects according to a logic of "inner" and "outer." To presume to see God as an item in one's own landscape—to pick God out, and represent God to oneself as a quantity one understands exhaustively—is, for Augustine, to make a mental representation of something, call it "God," locate it in one's mind, and then believe that one straightforwardly knows God. If there is a difference, it is difference in emphasis only, and not a point of disagreement. In any event, the sting of the worry is the same: the potential for an arrogant and overreaching human intellect to deem worthy of worship a product of its own activity.

At the same time, knowledge of the triune God must still be possible, or how can such a God be worshipped and loved? This worry haunts the Cappadocians, and certainly haunts Augustine. If we cannot pick God out as just another item accessible to human intellect, how can we know God at all? I see the Cappadocians, and Augustine, answering this question in ways whose placial implications are both similar and pneumatologically significant. Here Basil, the Gregories, and Augustine are concerned that presuming to locate God makes human intellect, so to speak, "fill all things." Human reason, in such an instance, acts as the master situater that is not itself situated; it marks off, delimits, circumscribes, and generates straightforward representations of all things, even God. This state of affairs is theologically disastrous because, of course, God must be confessed as the one who fills all things—marking off and delimiting the cosmos, creating and circumscribing and ordering all creatures. In the previous chapter, we encountered critiques of a definition of place having only to do with extension in domains. That critique is not explicitly indicated here, either for the Cappadocians or for Augustine. On the few occasions when place is thematized, for all the patristic interlocutors treated in this chapter, it does tend to indicate corporeal extension within the created domain. Mostly, less is said; place shows up just long enough for it to become clear that God is not placed, by which all four mean that God is not extended. So while it would be a mistake to portray these fourth-century theologians proto-Cartesians, neither (for example) are they proto-Bachelardians.

Yet certainly Basil and Augustine, and possibly also the Gregories to a lesser degree, indicate a kind of placial rehabilitation that is not altogether hostile to some of the insights of the modern and postmodern placial advocates. Such a rehabilitation will not put God into place—indeed, emphatically will not do so—but it will put certain things, which we can anachronistically call placial, into the trinitarian economy. What we postmodern readers might thematize as the placial aspects of experiential knowledge, are, for these theologians, situated by the trinitarian economy, which it is possible—under certain conditions—to imagine as a place. This trinitarian placing is sometimes christologically indicated, but often seems especially appropriate to the Spirit.

Basil of Caesarea

For Basil, Nyssen, and Nazianzen, and their contemporaries, to know something typically involves an activity of circumscription: picking out an intra-cosmic sensible or intelligible thing from among its surroundings, and understanding it through the conformation of mind to thing. But when faced with the Arian and semi-Arian heresies of the day—particularly those of the Eunomians—the Cappadocians qualify the scope of human knowledge in order to safeguard the divinity of the Son and the Spirit. Through appeals to causality and time, and by mapping the difference between "unbegotten" and "begotten" onto a difference in essence, the Eunomians argued that the Son was below the Father in rank and divinity. Unbegotten, they had contended, "circumscribed" the Father while begotten "circumscribed" the Son; this is true simply by virtue of how description and apprehension normally work. A difference is named, and therefore—according to the Eunomians—we are clearly talking about two different things: the unbegotten Father and the begotten Son. The ongoing hashing-out of the Son's status yielded a number of theological positions related to the divinity of Christ and Nicaea's famous *homoousios*: from those in the Nicene camp who disagreed over how and to what extent the Son was *homoousios* with the Father; to the semi-Arians who affirmed *homoousios* but, practically speaking, preferred to stress the differences between Father and Son; to the outright Arians who believed the Son to be a creature. Indeed, even the categories of "deity" and "creature"—and their scope—were under negotiation; and this may have been the most contested issue of all. As Ayres explains, the fourth century controversies were not a matter of asking "Are the Son and Spirit divine?" with one side answering "yes" and the other "no." Rather, at issue was the proper way to talk about divinity, and more than that, what sort of a property divinity is—whether it can be possessed in degrees, for example.[3]

As the controversy raged on, all parties realized that the status of the Spirit was very much a live issue too. Indeed, whoever managed to win the day on pneumatology would also be victorious on the matter of the Son.[4] For if the Spirit admitted semi-divinity, then the force of Nicene Christology—the force of *homoousios*—would be attenuated if not entirely undermined. Likewise if, through reflection on the Spirit, divinity proved to be all-or-nothing, then none of the arguments for a lesser Son could stand. Basil's status in securing the divinity of the Spirit—and therefore providing substantial parts of the foundation for the conceptual architecture of the trinity—is well established. As David Anderson observes, between 325 and 381, creedal confession proceeded from "We believe in the Holy Spirit" to "We believe in the Holy Spirit, the Lord, the Giver of Life, who proceeds from the Father; and who with the Father is worshipped and glorified." In between the two is Basil of Caesarea.[5]

At stake for Basil, among other things, was the liturgical language of the church. Not only did his Arian, semi-Arian, and Eunomian opponents presume to divide Father from Son from Spirit. They also presumed to divide up prepositions—in, through, with, etc.—and insist, for example, that a preposition like "through" is appropriate to the Son, who (they believed) mediates the Father's divinity to humanity while not exactly sharing in it to an equal degree. The Father, according to this logic, could be worshipped "through the Son" but not "with the Son." Likewise, the Father could be worshipped "in the Spirit" but not "with the Spirit." Among the many problems with this scheme, in Basil's eyes, is the fact that it contradicted many churches' liturgical practices, where prayers and baptisms either implied or outright used "with." Rhetorically, throughout *On the Holy Spirit*, Basil portrays his opponents as sowers of division. They divide churches from each other by casting doubt on established liturgical practices. They carefully parse and delineate their prepositions, specifying exactly which word

3. Ayres, "On Not Three People," 449.
4. Anderson, "Introduction," 11.
5. Ibid., 7.

may be used under which set of conditions, and which other word must be used under which other set of conditions. Most grievously of all, they divide Father from Son from Spirit. In fact, all of these divisions amounted to the same strategy, in Basil's eyes. The heretics' "old trick," Basil bemoans, is to act as though dissimilarity of words entails dissimilarity in fact. They act as if "things whose natures are dissimilar are expressed in dissimilar terms," unfailingly, and that the converse is true also: "dissimilar terms are used to describe things whose natures are dissimilar."[6]

What would account for such a crude and simplistic optimism towards human thought? Basil remarks that his opponents have been "led into this error . . . by their study of pagan writers."[7] And with that Basil embarks on what I see as a spatial dismantling, offering the faintest beginnings of a placial retrieval. Early in *On the Holy Spirit* Basil recites the Aristotelian typology of causes—final, efficient, material, formal. He also includes "time and place."[8] "Time and place," he explains, "might seem to contribute nothing to what is being produced, but outside them it would be impossible to make anything, since things are caused within the framework of place and time." The sting of Basil's critique lies in the accusation that his opponents have categorized God according to these categories. "Pagan philosophers... refer[red] to lifeless tools or the most abject work," he asserts, "but now Christians bind the Master of all with prepositions, and are not ashamed to describe the Creator of the universe with language fit for a hammer or a saw."[9] To do this is to take God—who is simple, and who transcends such distinctions—and introduce divisions, solely for the purpose of making God more comprehensible. The false god thus rendered manifests all the divisions of the divisive human intellect whose terms it meets. This god can be explained according to "[c]ause [which] has one nature, an instrument [which] has another, and place yet another."[10] A perverted pseudo-trinity emerges—with the Father as cause, the Son as instrument, and the Spirit as place—but full of divisions.

Created divisions—for Basil as for Nazianzen and Nyssen—entail frustration, competition, incompletion, exclusion. They simply cannot be internal to God. In this spirit Basil launches into the (very spatial) spoof of

6. Anderson, *St. Basil the Great On the Holy Spirit*, 18.
7. Ibid., 19.
8. Ibid., 19–20.
9. Ibid., 20.
10. Ibid., 22.

the only logical conclusion of his opponents' theological divisiveness: the Father and the Son fighting over a chair. "If they think," he mocks, "that the Son sits below the Father, in a lesser place, so that the Father sits above, and pushes the Son to the next seat below, let them say so, and we will be silent."[11] Here, again, a close connection emerges between place and epistemology—here having to do specifically with knowledge about God. Human knowledge operates according to divided causes, divided locations, divided vocabulary, and distension across space and time. To allow such reasoning to determine who God is—to demand that trinitarian thought accommodate itself to such divisions—is to require Father, Son, and Spirit to compete for that tiny plot of knowledge to which human reasoning holds the deed. Here the theological error becomes explicitly placial, for it contradicts divine omnipresence. "Anyone with a sound mind believes that God pervades everything," Basil points out, but those who oppose Father and Son "divide up from down." The fact that they have sneaked spatial division into their theological system belies, Basil suggests, their belief in the Father's incorporeality. Functionally, they locate Father and Son "in defined places," even though "[f]orm, shape, and bodily position cannot be invented for God[.]"[12]

Thus spatial and conceptual delimitation, and its close connection to the divisive tendencies of human knowledge, is a constant theme throughout *On the Holy Spirit*. Basil criticizes his opponents' tendency to subsume God to place, time, and causality. At the same time, Basil does not wish to invalidate the possibility of *any* sort of human knowledge about God. Given the deep connection between knowledge and location, might we not therefore assume that Basil theologically rehabilitates both?

"The goal of our calling," he writes, is "to become like God, as far as this is possible for human nature. But we cannot become like God unless we have knowledge of Him[?]"[13] Yet so often the unmoored pursuit of knowledge leads to the kind of self-indulgent philosophical conversations Basil has been lambasting—where participants vainly categorize and recategorize different sorts of causality and the kind of prepositions appropriate to each, and assume that God must fit within divisive and partial human concepts. Ultimately Basil affirms a kind of knowledge about God is possible—just as it is possible to make proper theological use of prepositions

11. Ibid., 30.
12. Ibid., 30–31.
13. Ibid., 16.

like "in," "through," and "with." What separates folly from piety—and what separates false circumscription from an appropriate sort of divine-human placing—is the acknowledgement of *human* delimitation and location. God fills all things; we are delimited and finite. If this is admitted, then certain placial terms can be readmitted as well, even if appended to God. *We* are placed *by God*—and specifically by the Holy Spirit.

Here he recalls the earlier, crudely rendered pseudo-trinity of his opponents—where the Father is the cause, the Son is the instrument, and the Spirit is the place. Concerning the Spirit's status as place, Basil turns his opponents argument against them; the Spirit, correctly understood, actually reverses the prideful human tendency to put God into a place, because the very name Spirit makes incorporeality evident in a way that refuses God's circumscription. "His first and most proper title," Basil asserts, "is Holy Spirit, a name most especially appropriate to everything which is incorporeal, purely immaterial, and indivisible"—all traits which human reasoning cannot comprehend. For this reason:

> . . . the Lord taught the Samaritan woman, who thought that God had to be worshipped in specific places, that "God is Spirit." He wanted to show that an incorporeal being cannot be circumscribed. When we hear the word "spirit" it is impossible for us to conceive of something whose nature can be circumscribed or is subject to change or variation. . . . Instead, we are compelled to direct our thoughts on high[.][14]

Notice the rhetorical contrast here. In one sense, the Spirit functions as a placial refusal—with the Spirit's "first and most proper title" exactly naming God's refusal to be circumscribed, in human thought, or in a location. Yet this very Spirit compels us to "direct our thoughts on high." Nor is this an isolated instance of positive placial language cropping up in the course of Basil's pneumatology. "[W]ho can listen to the Spirit's titles and not be lifted up in his soul?" Basil asks.[15] Basil refers to the Spirit as "tak[ing] . . . up His abode in someone's life."[16] Later he remarks that "[t]hrough the Holy Spirit comes our restoration to Paradise, our ascension to the Kingdom of heaven[.]"[17] Finally Basil makes it explicit. "Although paradoxical" he

---

14. Ibid., 42.
15. Ibid.
16. Ibid.
17. Ibid., 59.

says, "it is nevertheless true that Scripture frequently speaks of the Spirit in terms of *place*—a place *in* which people are made holy."[18]

Basil holds that it is both possible and appropriate to envision the Spirit as placing Christians, as placing the church—but only if one first roots out one's own presumptuous tendency to place and circumscribe God. Being placed "in the Spirit" therefore involves a humbling shift in one's understanding of knowledge itself. "This 'place,'" he explains, "is contemplation in the Spirit, and when Moses entered this 'place' God revealed Himself to him."[19] As an image, it coheres nicely with the Son's status as "door" or "way" which Basil had earlier discussed in chapter eight. These titles are not predicated according to the divine nature or essence, but according to the divine energies—those means "by which [God] satisfies the needs of each in His tenderheartedness to His creation."[20] The Spirit is not the place of the Father and Son—"it is more appropriate to say that [the Spirit] dwells *with* them"[21]—but as a place within the trinitarian economy of redemption. In other words, the Spirit places us; and by placing us, allows us to perceive the limited scope of our own finite, circumscribing manner of knowing and placing. "To worship *in* the Spirit implies that our intelligence has been enlightened[,]" not least about its own finite scope.[22]

Other features of place remain, however: directionality, navigability, and dwelling. For here is an underlying logic of ascent and descent in Basil's thought; believers, once "inseparably joined to the Spirit of knowledge[,]" are "led up" through the Son to the Father.[23] This movement is initiated by the descending divine activity it mirrors: the Father's manifestation in the Son, which is communicated by the sending-down of the Spirit of truth.[24] Indwelling abounds—but in ways that confound the calculus of circum-

---

18. Anderson, *St. Basil the Great On the Holy Spirit*, 94; also given (with translation of "chora") in Bobrinskoy, "Indwelling of the Spirit of Christ," 57.

19. Anderson, *St. Basil the Great On the Holy Spirit*, 95.

20. Ibid., 36.

21. Ibid., 95.

22. Ibid., 97.

23. Ibid., 74.

24. See especially Anderson, *St. Basil the Great On the Holy Spirit*, 65 (Basil's 16, 32). Bobrinksoy points out that the same logic is evident in Basil's *Against Heresies*, in which Basil describes "the movement and the pattern of ascension of those who are saved: they ascend through the Spirit to the Son, and through the Son to the Father, and at the end the Son will yield up his work to the Father." Basil, *Against Heresies*, V.36.2, quoted in Bobrinskoy, "Indwelling of the Spirit of Christ," 55.

scription and delimitation. On the one hand "[t]he Spirit is indeed the dwelling-place of the saints," but at the same time "the saint is a suitable abode for the Spirit, since he has supplied God with a house, and is called a temple of God."[25] Spirit and saint co-inhere, each dwelling in the other, effecting a bridging of difference. If the heretics would subsume God to place—thereby circumscribing God and introducing division—the Spirit accomplishes precisely the opposite, in ways that evoke place without subsuming God to place.

To be sure, *On the Holy Spirit* is not the only work of Basil's whose theological themes and arguments pertain to place. In the *Hexaemeron* Basil's meditation upon the ordering of the cosmos took sharp polemical aim at philosophical sophistry and hubris, but in an innovative and revealing way. Isaac Miller suggests that Basil went further than Philo did in *De opificio mundi*, and indeed stretched the genre conventions of hexaemeral commentary. For Basil, "[t]he natural world was not simply the object about which philosophical debates were waged; it was a participant in these debates, the key to its polemical position being contained in the literal meaning of Genesis."[26] This polemical tone emerges as early as his gloss on Genesis 1.1 in the first homily. "'In the beginning God created the heaven and the earth.' I stop struck with admiration at this thought. What shall I first say? Where shall I begin my story? Shall I show forth the vanity of the Gentiles?"[27] The very cosmos argue against the pagan creation accounts which Basil quickly runs through—the arguments of those "philosophers of Greece [who] have made much ado to explain nature" through emanationism or atomism or causality—all "because they knew not how to say 'In the beginning God created the heaven and the earth.'"[28] Basil further suggests that these philosophical tendencies accompany an affective tendency towards an unwholesome fascination with the material world. In the third homily, in the reflection on Genesis 1:8—"And God called the firmament heaven"—Basil compares the beauty of the scriptural account of heaven to that of a "chaste woman [which] surpasses that of the harlot," which he in turn likens to "the inquisitive discussion of philosophers" and

25. Anderson, *St. Basil the Great On the Holy Spirit*, 95.
26. Miller, "Idolatry and the Polemics of World-Formation from Philo to Augustine," 137.
27. Basil of Caesarea, "The Hexaemeron," Homily 1, section 2, in Schaff and Wace, *Nicene and Post-Nicene Fathers, Second Series*, vol. 8.
28. Ibid.

their speculation about heaven.[29] And in the fifth homily, Basil goes so far as to say that God chose the third day for the "adornment of the earth" with grants and plants, with an eye to ruling out heliolatry, "that those who worship the sun, as the source of life, may renounce their error."[30] Of course, the more predominant theme in the *Hexaemeron* is not how the cosmos refute theological error, but how they display theological truth. The cosmos displays God's wise and intricate arrangement of creatures and their respective powers, activities, and environments—a theme we shall shortly see put to use in Gregory Nazianzen's Theological Orations.

Thus, although I lack the space for an extended treatment of Basil's *Hexaemeron*, these very sparse quotations indicate a complementary view of place to that used in *On the Holy Spirit*. Revealed knowledge has what we might—somewhat anachronistically, but not entirely anachronistically—call a placial aspect. This holds whether one is considering the place-like activity of the Spirit through which the believer is brought to knowledge about God, as seen in *On the Holy Spirit*. It also holds when one the activity of the cosmos itself which—thanks to God's providential ordering in the act of creation—actually refutes theological error.

Gregory of Nazianzus

In Gregory of Nazianzus' Theological Orations, the placial elements are somewhat more muted than in Basil's *On the Holy Spirit,* although they are not absent. The epistemological elements, though, come out in full force. As Beeley notes, although the Theological Orations constitute Nazianzen's most famous trinitarian defense, he "begins not with ideas about God, Christ, or the Holy Spirit, but with a rhetorically charged prologue that focuses on the reader's own character and attitude about God, in order to establish the human conditions for the possibility of knowing God."[31] Early

---

29. Basil, "The Hexaemeron," Homily 3, section 8, in Schaff and Wace, *Nicene and Post-Nicene Fathers, Second Series*, vol. 8. As Miller notes, this strikes a different chord than that struck by Augustine in his anti-Manichean writings, in which "Augustine noted in opposition . . . that God took 'pleasure' at his own creation. This exegetical reference reversed the message of Basil's sexual metaphor to warn off the sensuous attachments of the natural philosophers. Divine pleasure, rather than chaste indifference, was the affective model for human contemplation of the cosmos," Miller, "Idolatry and the Polemics of World-Formation from Philo to Augustine," 139.

30. Basil, "The Hexaemeron," Homily 5, section 1, in Schaff and Wace, *Nicene and Post-Nicene Fathers, Second Series*, vol. 8.

31. Beeley, *Gregory of Nazianzus on the Trinity and the Knowledge of God*, 65.

on Nazianzen stipulates that knowledge of God does not belong to any thoughtful person whatsoever, but rather to those "who have been previously purified in soul and body, or at the very least are being purified."[32] Even if one has the proper philosophizers, the other conditions might be wrong. "Not before every audience, nor at all times, nor on all points" can one speculate about God, but only "on certain occasions, and before certain persons, and within certain limits[.]"[33]

The need for such discretion stems from our tendency to distort things by making them fit the conditions that are easy for us—as creatures possessing both sense and intellect—to impose. Conversely, what we apprehend can overwhelm us—as too much light can overwhelm an eye. Moreover, when such distortions are directed at God, it is (to put it mildly) self-serving. Not only is it easy—in a sloppy and haphazard sense—to set up (for example) the sun as a deity, Nazianzen suggests; but it sets up the human knower as a connoisseur of divinity. Therefore, knowing God involves purifying one's intellect of that habit into which human beings lapse with frightening ease—namely, taking our own finite sense-perception as the measure and revealer of all that is. From this it follows that part of knowing God is to realize that one will never exactly know God, certainly not in the way one knows another finite creature. Thus in the Second Theological Oration Nazianzen offers the "opinion [that] it is impossible to express [God], and yet more impossible to conceive him" because the "thick covering of the flesh is an obstacle to the full understanding of the truth."[34] It is not that human reasoning is worthless, or natural theology entirely wrongheaded. After all, "our very eyes and the law of nature teach us that God exists and that he is the efficient and maintaining cause of all things." With our senses—sight in particular—we perceive "visible objects," their "beautiful stability and progress," and thereby perceive "natural law, because through these visible things and their order it reasons back to their author."[35] Nazianzen does not merely permit this sort of thinking, but recommends it. Recognition of the basic intelligibility and beauty of creation and its laws is essential for

---

32. Gregory of Nazianzus, "First Theological Oration," section 3, in Hardy, *Christology of the Later Fathers,* 129.

33. Ibid.

34. Gregory of Nazianzus, "Second Theological Oration," section 4, in ibid., 138.

35. Gregory of Nazianzus, "Second Theological Oration," section 6, in ibid., 139.

understanding God as creator, "[A]nd very wanting is sense is he who will not willingly go thus far in following natural proofs[.]"[36]

The rules change, though, when humans attempt to know God. "Who ever reached this extremity of wisdom?"[37] he asks. As with Basil, separation and circumscription serve as hallmarks of finite, embodied knowledge. To overlay any of these onto God is to imply that God is both corporeal (because delimited) and divisible (because corporeal). In other words, to subsume God's identity to human reason, to bring God under humanity's purview—even unintentionally, even out of habit—is implicitly to affirm all of these traits of God. For such are the "approximations of reason[.]" Reason identifies circumscribable bodies, finite things, things that can be divided into parts and classified. "[W]hat will you conceive the Deity to be," asks Nazianzen, "if you rely upon [these] approximations[?] . . . [H]ow is he an object of worship if he be circumscribed? Or how shall he escape being made of elements, and therefore subject to be resolved into them again, or even altogether dissolved?"[38]

Nazianzen's point, like Basil's, is that the Eunomian logic only holds if Father, Son, and Spirit are appropriate quantities for human reasoning to exercise its powers upon. If they are—if "Father" and "Son" function like "table" and "chair"—then indeed the terms "begotten" and "unbegotten" would indicate that Father and Son are two discrete entities. But that is hardly a theologically joyous outcome, suggests Nazianzen. For it implies that division—not only division between Father and Son, but also division between *all* entities that facilitates their being mentally circumscribed—wins the day. No happy fate, when one considers what division ultimately admits: "For every compound is a starting point of strife, and strife of separation, and separation of dissolution."[39] This is true of corporeal things, but Nazianzen's point is that his opponents are treating God as a corporeal thing by treating God as a quantity upon which finite human reasoning operates perfectly. This contradicts other basic assumptions about God which all parties to the debate would have shared—that "God is boundless (*apeiron*), limitless (*aoriston*), formless (*aschêmatiston*), impalpable (*anaphes*) and invisible (*aoraton*), since all these properties are incompatible with the no-

---

36. Ibid., 140.

37. Ibid.

38. Gregory of Nazianzus, "Second Theological Oration," section 7, in Hardy, *Christology of the Later Fathers*, 140

39. Ibid.

Patristic Precedents

tion of body."[40] If we exclude these from the notion of body in God's special case, then either we are no longer talking about something about which finite concepts and thoughts no longer straightforwardly apply (which is Nazianzen's claim); or else we are talking about a body that is especially lacking—because it shows up nowhere and has no form. Furthermore, if God is a body, then eventually God will suffer separation (*diastasis*) and dissolution (*lusis*).[41]

Nazianzen's rhetoric implies that his Eunomian opponents are masters of division, separation, and dissolution: they divide Father, Son, and Spirit; they divide the church; and all because they allow human reason—with its finite, fleshy habit of separating corporeal things from each other so as to understand them—free reign. Given half a chance they would introduce theological misunderstandings that threaten to dissolve the very God they claim to worship. Happily, asserts Nazianzen, they are incorrect, and God is *not* corporeal or divisible or circumscribable, "[f]or no inspired teacher has yet asserted or admitted such a notion[.]" If the lexical distinction between "begotten" and "unbegotten" confounds human reasoning, then that is because human reasoning is finite; not because either Father or Son can be divided and circumscribed. In section ten, the discussion of God's indivisibility, lack of circumscription and (especially) incorporeality naturally turns to a question about God's place. "Now that we have ascertained that God is incorporeal," remarks Gregory, it is time to "proceed a little further" and ask, "Is [God] nowhere or somewhere?" If God is nowhere, he continues, then how can one even say that God exists? On the other hand, if God is somewhere, God must be in the universe—either the whole universe, or just a part of it—or in some domain above the universe, which (according to Nazianzen) makes little sense. On what basis would one posit a domain "above" the universe but not include it in the universe? And in any case, he continues, if God's location is the universe then where was God before the universe was created.[42]

To this, Nazianzen offers something of a non-answer, but it is an instructive non-. The question itself is nonsensical, he explains, which is precisely why he raised it in the first place. "[M]y purpose in doing so[,]" he explains, was "to make clear the point at which my argument has aimed

40. Narkevics, "Skiagraphia," 87.

41. Ibid.

42. Gregory of Nazianzus, "Second Theological Oration," section 10, in Hardy, *Christology of the Later Fathers*, 142.

from the first." Simply put, the fact that one cannot even make sense of the question "Is God nowhere or somewhere?" suggests an important theological truth: "[t]hat the divine nature cannot be apprehended by human reason, and that we cannot even represent to ourselves all its greatness."[43] Believers must always keep this fact in mind, Nazianzen urges, for human reason is lazy. Frankly, our intellects find it much easier to generate a circumscribable, comprehensible, separable, compound, extended, and located God. Nazianzen is haunted by this ease with which human intellects do this. He speculates as to why a good God would have made it so difficult to know the true God, and so easy to lapse into imagining false gods. Perhaps, he speculates, it was because we tend to care more about things won after much difficulty. Or perhaps God intended to spare human beings the fate of Lucifer, for whom apprehension of God's "full light" was an occasion for the fall. Or perhaps God means to reward all the more greatly those who have persevered despite the distorting tendencies of their mental powers.[44] But this, he says resignedly, is our lot. "[O]ur mind faints to transcend corporeal things, and to consort with the incorporeal," but such longings remain unfulfilled. This same mind, which cannot conceive of anything "apart from motion and diffusion," must resign itself to looking "with its inherent weakness at things above its strength."[45]

Moreover, the weakness of the human intellect affects how human beings view the cosmos. Despite the fact that Nazianzen began the Second Theological Oration by acknowledging the legitimacy of natural theology, beginning with section thirteen he discusses how even regarding the cosmos can be an occasion for danger. Not only do we all too easily make God into what amounts to a corporeal entity, but we also tend to make corporeal entities into gods. Many people, Nazianzen reminds his opponents, divinize elements of the cosmos, making "a god of the sun, others of the moon, others of the host of stars, others of the heavens itself . . . [and others] any chance visible objects, setting up the most beautiful of what they saw as their gods."[46] Again, people do this because it is easy, whereas "the truth . . . is full of difficulty and obscurity."[47]

---

43. Gregory of Nazianzus, "Second Theological Oration," section 11, in ibid., 143.
44. Gregory of Nazianzus, "Second Theological Oration," section 12, in ibid., 144.
45. Gregory of Nazianzus, "Second Theological Oration," section 13, in ibid., 144–45.
46. Gregory of Nazianzus, "Second Theological Oration," section 14, in ibid., 145.
47. Gregory of Nazianzus, "Second Theological Oration," section 21, in ibid., 150.

Patristic Precedents

Yet the concluding sections of the Second Theological Oration still contains the hint of a placial retrieval following a placial disavowal—although it is not hinted at so strongly as the retrieval Basil's *On the Holy Spirit*. For in those concluding sections, Nazianzen embarks upon a lengthy meditation upon the cosmos, in all its beautiful and well-ordered differentiation. In sections 22-31 Nazianzen embarks upon a lengthy meditation upon the divine skill and wisdom with which planetary motion, elemental activity, animal and plant life, sound and light, and human existence are arranged—excluding not even "the fishy tribe gliding through the waters" nor the "tribes of birds"[48] nor the "gulfs of the sea bound together with one another and with the land"[49]; nor the fact that "the earth stands solid and unswerving"; nor "all the great height of mountains, and the various clefts of its coast line cut off from it[.]""Tell me[,]" he asks, "how and whence are these things? What is this great web unwrought by art?" The order and beauty of the cosmos "are no less worthy of admiration in respect of their mutual relations than when considered separately."[50] The appreciation of the cosmos—in their intricate entirety, and in their capacity to make manifest the divine wisdom behind creation—is, Nazianzen implies, an appropriate way to appreciate that domain in which human intellects find themselves. A finite, divisive, and proud human intellect will presume to divide this wise arrangement, affording no praise to the one "in accordance with which the universe is moved and controlled."[51] It will zero in on one or a few discrete created items or processes as being divine, thereby sneakily enjoying the flattering implication that it has managed to pinpoint divinity. Again, one notes the function of separation in Nazianzen's Theological Orations; the impulse, which would circumscribe and separate the Word and Spirit from the divinity of the Father, is the same proud impulse which would separate one component of the cosmos and worship it—failing to worship the triune God, and failing to appreciate the divine wisdom that orders the entire cosmos in all its vast and intricate design.

For Nazianzen, though, pneumatology and place do not intensify each other in the way they do for Basil. We would look for such an intensification in the third through fifth theological orations, in which Nazianzen explicates his Christology and pneumatology further. Place does not show up

48. Gregory of Nazianzus, "Second Theological Oration," section 24, in ibid., 152.
49. Gregory of Nazianzus, "Second Theological Oration," section 24, in ibid., 154.
50. Gregory of Nazianzus, "Second Theological Oration," section 26, in ibid.
51. Gregory of Nazianzus, "Second Theological Oration," section 16, in ibid., 147.

as an especially apt pneumatological metaphor as it does for Basil, because Nazianzen's pneumatological stakes were different than Basil's. As Beeley argues, although Basil—like Gregory of Nazianzus—had contrasted the active lordship of the Spirit with the bondage of creatures, Basil did not forcefully and straightforwardly identify the Spirit as God.[52] Nazianzen makes precisely this assertion, and forcefully. "Is the Spirit God?" he asks. "Most certainly. Well then, is He consubstantial? Yes, if He is God."[53] One could speculate that, for Nazianzen, the pneumatological metaphor of place did not particularly suit his case for (in Beeley's words) a "sharp ontological divide" between God and creatures that "admits of no intermediate, third status of being."[54]

Recall that Nazianzen is ever sounding the alarm whenever finite language threatens to insert divisions between the persons. He does so in his Christology, when he asserts that "monarchy is that which we hold in honor. It is, however, a monarchy that is not limited to one person, for it is possible for a unity if at variance with itself to come into a condition of plurality[.]"[55] To introduce divisions between Father, Son and Spirit—as he suggests the Eunomians have done—is to posit a unity at variance with itself, an extrinsic unity which might cease. To protect against this one must posit an "equality of nature, and a union of mind, and an identity of motion, and a convergence of its elements to unity—a thing which is impossible to the created nature[.]"[56] He sounds the alarm, as well, in the fifth theological oration on the Spirit. "For one is not more and another less God; nor is one before and another after; nor are they divided in will or parted in power; nor can you find here any of the qualities of divisible things[,]" he emphasizes. None of these factors—degree, time, will, power, divisibility—attach to Father, Son, and Spirit. When we consider God from the standpoint of "Godhead, or first cause, or the monarchia" we conceive a God without any of these divisions. Only when we consider "the Persons in whom the Godhead dwells" are there three.[57]

52. Beeley, *Gregory of Nazianzus on the Trinity and the Knowledge of God*, 162.

53. Gregory of Nazianzus, "Fifth Theological Oration," section 10, in Hardy, *Christology of the Later Fathers*, 199.

54. Beeley, *Gregory of Nazianzus on the Trinity and the Knowledge of God*, 162.

55. Gregory of Nazianzus, "Third Theological Oration," 2 in Hardy, *Christology of the Later Fathers*, 161.

56. Ibid.

57. Gregory of Nazianzus, "Fifth Theological Oration," 14 in Hardy, *Christology of the Later Fathers*, 202.

Patristic Precedents

One can see how, if Nazianzen is trying to prove a shared *monarchia*, it does not suit his case to invoke the metaphor of Spirit as place. Moreover, the bulk of the fifth theological oration he addresses at length his opponents' charge that, because scripture nowhere says that the Spirit is consubstantial with the Father and the Son, it is improper to say so.[58] His answer here barely flirts with placiality. When Nazianzen does find metaphors for how the Spirit dwells with us as part of God's saving activity, the metaphors are both temporal and placial. Gregory likens the missions of the three persons to three successive "earthquakes," the first "from idols to the Law," the second "from the law to the gospel," and the third "from this earth to that which cannot be shaken or moved."[59] These changes happen in time, first, because finite creatures could be overwhelmed beyond their capacities by a simultaneous revelation; and, second, because it suited God to move us "by persuasion" rather than by force.[60] This dynamic accounts for the fact that the Spirit's divine, consubstantial status is not straightforwardly explained in scripture. For while [t]he Old Testament proclaimed the Father openly, and the Son more obscurely[,]" and "[t]he New manifested the Son, and suggested the Deity of the Spirit[,]" presently "the Spirit Himself dwells among us, and supplies us with a clearer demonstration of Himself."[61] The point of this claim—to explain why the Spirit's consubstantial divinity is not explicated in scripture—relies on its being temporal, and not only metaphorically so. There are also, however, placial whispers: the analogy to earthquakes, the assertion that the Spirit dwells with us, and the suggestion that the Spirit's role is to bring us from this earth to a realm which cannot be shaken.

Too, there is the Spirit's role in our understanding and perception. Nazianzen argues that part of the Spirit's role in dwelling with us is to teach "the Deity of the Spirit Himself," at a time "when such knowledge should be seasonable and capable of being received after our Saviour's restoration, when it would no longer be received with incredulity because of its marvellous character."[62] The Spirit's role as teacher—made possible by Christ—in

---

58. See Beeley, *Gregory of Nazianzus on the Trinity and the Knowledge of God*, 168 for a lengthy discussion on Nazianzen's tactics here.

59. Gregory of Nazianzus, "Fifth Theological Oration," 25 in Hardy, *Christology of the Later Fathers*, 208.

60. Ibid., 209.

61. Gregory of Nazianzus, "Fifth Theological Oration," 26 in ibid.

62. Gregory of Nazianzus, "Fifth Theological Oration," 27 in ibid., 210.

turn makes possible the sort of purification and illumination whereby theological knowledge is possible, the very claim with which Nazianzen had begun his theological orations. Like Basil, Nazianzen envisions this process of purification and illumination as like being "lifted up," and also like acquiring more light by which to see.[63] So creaturely sense, intellect, apprehension and finitude all converge on the Spirit's manner of dwelling—even if Nazianzen gives this a more strongly temporal gloss, and even if he is less emphatic than Basil in likening the Spirit to the place in which believers are made holy.

Gregory of Nyssa

Many elements of Nyssen's thought are shared by Basil or Nazianzen or both. Because of this, I shall primarily—and all too briefly—focus here on those elements of Nyssen's work which I find most promising for a constructive trinitarian theology of place. First, I shall discuss the role of aroundness in Nyssen's thought, and the fact that it sounds in both the trinitarian and epistemological registers. In the course of discussing aroundness, I shall also discuss Nyssen's contention that the trinity is without interval or distention. Finally, I shall flag Nyssen's equation of the term "godhead" with God's activity of beholding and overseeing the cosmos—although I confess I am not yet sure what the placial implications of this last might be.

Gregory claims that descriptive terms for God do not describe God's essence, but "rather they describe things 'around' (*peri*) the divine nature, things through which the divine nature may be known."[64] Thus such terms take on a special sense (*idian dianoian*), which work only because some feature of our world reflects God's activity. By negating or intensifying the feature in question, one may attempt to speak worthily of God. Such conceptions (*epinoia*) never refer to the divine essence directly—nor could any human capacity ever do so, given our weak capacity. Nevertheless, they are appropriate, because they take as their point of departure God's own self-revelation in creation.[65]

Nyssen also uses the term *periphera* (as well as *anakyklosis*) to evoke a rotating movement of the three persons around each other in the godhead. Naturally such aroundness is incorporeal and nonphysical. "Surely[,]"

63. Beeley, *Gregory of Nazianzus on the Trinity and the Knowledge of God*, 118–19.
64. Ayres, "On Not Three People," 456.
65. Ibid.

Nyssen scoffs in *Contra Eunomium*, "no one is such a child in understanding so as mentally to superimpose concepts of spatial differentiation upon intellectual and incorporeal nature, for position in space is proper to bodies[.]"[66] To the contrary, the way in which the Persons are both around each other, and in each other, "is recognized to be far outside the domain of spatial concepts."[67] Nor is aroundness the only spatialized language with which one might evoke the relationship of the three persons. Indeed, mutual interiority is another, very important, spatial and placial image. Stramara observes the way in which the Johannine "in" becomes a handy weapon for Nyssen against Eunomius. Again, this is familiar Cappadocian territory. Because the Persons contain each other fully, "the One in his entirety, entirely in the Other; the Father not superabounding in the Son, nor the Son diminishing in the Father[,]"[68] Eunomius is therefore wrong to circumscribe Father and Son with the terms "unbegotten" and "begotten"—and not only because circumscription is appropriate to bodily things only.[69] Even if one wanted to delimit God, one would find the Son already, so to speak, inside the Father and the Father inside the Son. God is therefore *adiastaton*—without interval—in two senses. God is not extended in space, as a body is; but nor is there any interval between the three persons.[70] Indeed, the interval which Gregory believes we ought to be mindful of is that "huge and infinite . . . middle-wall" which separates "Uncreated Being vis-à-vis the created existence. The latter is bounded, the former has no boundary. The latter can . . . be comprehended; of the former, the measure is infinity [and] exceeds all dimensional understanding[.]"[71] As Verghese

66. Gregory of Nyssa, *Contra Eunomium* 1.15 cited (n.10) in Stramara, "Gregory of Nyssa's Terminology for Trinitarian Perichoresis," 257.

67. Gregory of Nyssa, *Contra Eunomium* 1.15 in Stramara, "Gregory of Nyssa's Terminology for Trinitarian Perichoresis," 258.

68. Gregory of Nyssa, *Refutatio confessionis Eunomii*, (CE 2.4), GNO 2 322, 27—323, 2; in Stramara, "Gregory of Nyssa's Terminology for Trinitarian Perichoresis," 259 (see n. 215).

69. The argument that circumscription is appropriate to bodily things, but not to God, also dominates in Nyssen's thought as it did in Basil's and Nazianzen's. See, for example, "On Not Three Gods" in Hardy, *Christology of the Later Fathers*, 264: "Only those things are enumerated by addition which are seen to be individually circumscribed. This circumscription is noted by bodily appearance, by size, by place, and by distinction of form and color."

70. Verghese, "*Diastema* and *Diastasis* in Gregory of Nyssa: Introduction to a Concept and the Posing of a Problem," 249.

71. Ibid., 253, quoting Gregory of Nyssa, Contra Eunomius, chapter II, section 69ff.

notes, Nyssen's way of framing *diastema* here points to a paradox; ordinarily the word would refer to a gap between two points, a boundary applying to one in the same manner as the other. Here, there is a boundary, but it applies only to one of the parties: creation.[72] It does not apply to God, since God "transcends the created order, being beyond all diastematic conception [and] surpass[ing] all temporal . . . reasoning[.]"[73] The "middle wall" between God and creation is thus the boundary of human thought itself, delimiting finite intellects and thereby determining their circumscribing powers, but exercising no such power on God.[74]

All this is indicated by speaking of the coinherence of the three Persons. While it is appropriate to speak thus—under the aspect of *epinoia*—it does not designate the divine essence nor actual spatiality. If the Persons' coinherence confounds our spatial categories, Nyssen suggests, then we rightly conclude that our spatial categories are finite and creaturely. But what of the Persons' aroundness? Here we find hints of a connection between pneumatology and placiality. In *Adversus Macedonianos* Nyssen exhorts the reader to " . . . see the revolving circle of the glory moving round (*periphoran*) . . . from Like to Like. The Son is glorified by the Spirit; the Father is glorified by the Son; again the Son possesses glory from the Father; and the only-begotten becomes the glory of the Spirit."[75] This passage comes on the heels of Nyssen's remark that the Spirit searches the depths of God.[76] Glory tracks closely with what we—again, under the aspect of *epinoia*—perceive and describe as the aroundness of the Persons to each other. The glory each person gives to the other two renders their relationships non-static, revolving, whirling, always encompassing the others.[77] One wonders whether this *periphera* correlates with the aroundness—the uniquely approximating characteristic—of human knowledge about God. Permit me to flag this possibility; and to suggest that, if it is the case, then it would prove a very useful element for constructing a contemporary trinitarian theology of place. Again, though, danger abounds; one

(Verghese's translation).

72. Ibid., 254.

73. *Contra Eunomium* I 363–64, quoted in ibid..

74. Ibid., 255.

75. Gregory of Nyssa, *Adversus Maconianos*, GNO 3.1 109, 7–15, in Stramara, "Gregory of Nyssa's Terminology for Trinitarian Perichoresis," 260.

76. Stramara, "Gregory of Nyssa's Terminology for Trinitarian Perichoresis," 260.

77. Ibid., 260–61.

must ever keep in mind that "middle wall" which bounds human intellection but exercises no such boundary on God. The aroundness of *epinoia* would have to derive entirely from God's self-revelation—a self-revelation which (to we finite humans) looks a bit like three Persons whirling around each other, glorifying each other, tracing each others' boundaries, and containing each other. The thinking could not run in the other direction; one could not spatialize or corporealize God's *periphoran* simply to meet the specifications of creatures in their finitude. Bearing this in mind, it makes sense that *periphera* would be offset by mutual inclusion, by *perichoresis*— a noun not put to trinitarian use by Nyssen, but (according to Stramara) nonetheless indicated in his thought.[78]

Another fascinating placial datum—in light of the previous chapter's thinkers' emphasis upon the beholding aspects of place—is Nyssen's argument that the term "godhead" refers not to God's nature but to God's activity of beholding and overseeing the cosmos. In "On Not Three Gods" Gregory asserts that nothing, not even the word "Godhead" refers directly to the divine nature itself, for "every name, whether invented by human custom or handed down by the Scriptures, is indicative of our conceptions" of God's nature but "does not signify what that nature is in itself."[79] Nyssen suggests that perhaps Godhead (*theotēs*) "is derived from 'beholding' (*thea*)" indicating that God "oversees all things . . . and is called the overseer of the universe" for "to behold and to see are the same thing[.]"[80] Nyssen's point here is that this power, this operation of overseeing, cannot be divided according to the Persons. With creatures, individuals sharing a nature can perform the same operation while still being individuated differently—even as the natures themselves remain shared. With God, the shared operation of beholding indicates a unity more profound than that of individual creatures who share a nature.[81] It constitutes "one motion and disposition[:]"[82] the Father "exercises his power of overseeing or beholding . . . through the Only-begotten, who by the Holy Spirit makes all power perfect[.]"[83]

78. Ibid., 255.
79. Gregory of Nyssa, "On Not Three Gods," in Hardy, *Christology of the Later Fathers*, 259.
80. Ibid.
81. This is one of the main points of Ayres' analysis in "On Not Three People."
82. Gregory of Nyssa, "On Not Three Gods," in Hardy, 262.
83. Ibid., 263.

But power brings us, again, to aroundness. According to Ayres, Gregory here draws upon Plotinus' understanding of power being (metaphorically) "around" a nature, a sort of "surrounding reality directed to what is outside"[84] which is distinct from the nature itself. For Nyssen, this Plotinian sense of aroundness indicates God's activity in the world—the economy, as is the shorthand. The pertinent distinction is between knowing the power of a nature, and knowing the nature.[85] Putting all of Nyssen's placial and spatial metaphors together, what we get—if I understand correctly—is something like this: God's nature is unknown, but God's power—which is metaphorically "around" the nature and directed toward creation—reveals godself. Meanwhile, human knowers know "around" God through *epinoia*, made possible through ascetic practice and gradual illumination by the Holy Spirit. This illumination makes it possible to "see" God rightly—though, again, the divine nature itself is inaccessible. One of the things that the human knower, so illuminated, may see is a God who (so to speak) also "sees," whose inner life entails something like three persons whirlingly moving around each other while dwelling in each other.

In other words, there is a consonance between two entirely different orders of reality. On the one hand, human creatures uniquely engage with sensible and intelligible reality, and in so doing we locate things around us: we see things (provided there is adequate light to do so), we note their features, we look around them, we see what they do. On the other hand—and here speaking only "around" the quantity in question—God beholds all; the Persons are in and around each other; and this very power is available for our finite apprehension only because God has revealed it to be so. Moreover, this entire schema holds only because of the inviolable middle wall firmly delimiting creation but not delimiting God. If I understand this model correctly, it goes rooting place in triunity without succumbing the trinity to place. It may even admit a more contemporary understanding of place, having to do not with extension so much as with meaning and navigability. Indeed, given Nyssen's—and all the Cappadocians'—concern for theological epistemology, the connection seems an easy one.

---

84. Ayres, "On Not Three People," 458.
85. Ibid.

Patristic Precedents

Augustine of Hippo

Earlier I suggested that the placial logic of Augustine's trinitarian theology may reveal a difference in sensibility between him and the Cappadocians. In the section that remains I shall try to support that claim—while also arguing that the difference ultimately makes rather less difference than we might expect. Aroundness, periphery and circumscription are, I contend, less central to Augustine's trinitarian thought; he prefers to place the trinitarian relations according to "inner" and "outer." (This, of course, is different than saying that Augustine offers a comprehensive doctrine of interiority as such; or that Augustine uses these terms literally or without theological qualification.) I do not mean thereby to take a position on the larger issues of whether and how Augustine's trinitarian theology departs from Cappadocian trinitarian theology; whether and how this signals a fundamental difference between the Eastern and Western theological inheritance; or which model is superior (if indeed the differences go that deep). In particular, the careful parsing of "person" and "relation," and the ways in which they are differently inflected for Augustine versus Nazianzen and Nyssen, is—while important—outside of the placial focus of this dissertation.[86] I do, however, offer the following analysis as a possible data point in the larger debate.

In book 7 of the *Confessions,* Augustine details a shift in his understanding of God. Notably, it is a shift away from a crudely spatialized understanding. As a Manichean, Augustine recalls, he believed that "[w]hatever was not stretched out in space, or diffused or compacted or inflated or possessed of some such qualities, or at least capable of possessing them, I judged to be nothing at all."[87] Charles Taylor argues, in *Sources of the Self,* that Augustine was a proto-Cartesian because (according to Taylor) he grounds knowledge in reflexive self-understanding.[88] I suggest, to the contrary, that any suggestion of a proto-Cartesian element in

---

86. See LaCugna, *God for Us,* particularly chapter 3, "Augustine and the Trinitarian Economy of the Soul"; and Zizioulas, *Being as Communion.* LaCugna and Zizioulas argue that Augustine defines trinitarian personhood in such a way as to divorce personhood from relationship to other divine persons, resulting in a substantialist metaphysic that pervades his theological system, in turn conferring this habit to the western theological tradition. In contrast, Ayres argues against such a distinction in (among other places) chapter 15 of *Nicaea and Its Legacy* and in *Augustine and the Trinity.*

87. Augustine *Confessions* 7 (Boulding, 121).

88. See Taylor chapter 7, "In Interiore Homine" (127–42), especially Taylor's suggestion that "Augustine anticipated Descartes" with "a sort of proto-cogito" (141).

59

The Place of the Spirit

Augustine's thought would more properly be located here. Augustine, on his own account, allows material extension to exhaustively determine possibilities for location. But Augustine recalls that "in so thinking I was gross of heart and not even luminous to myself[.]" It is important to note, here, what Augustine says about his own sense of sight, and his misinterpretation thereof. Because his eyes—which one would think could operate properly with adequate light—"were accustomed to roam among material forms," Augustine's error (so he tells us) was in neglecting the role of perception in making mental images. In other words, because his eyes only saw material forms, Augustine erroneously concluded that all reality must be material. He "could not see that this very act of perception, whereby I formed those images, was different from them in kind[.]"[89]

Again, epistemology, perception and placiality reinforce each other—though trinity is not yet indicated. Nevertheless, Augustine's misconceptions are not without theological ramifications. He recalls, "I thought that even you, Life of my life, were a vast reality spread throughout space in every direction: I thought that you penetrated the whole mass of earth and the immense, unbounded spaces beyond it on all sides[.]" Interestingly, even at this early point Augustine appreciates the force of the claim that limitation applies to creatures only; he writes that he believed creatures "found their limits in you, while you yourself had no limit anywhere." Of course, Augustine realizes in retrospect that such a schema must be false, since "on that showing a larger part of the earth would contain a larger portion of you, and a smaller a lesser portion,"[90] and Augustine finds the notion of greater and lesser shares of divinity unacceptable. Augustine later relates how he was disabused of this inadequate understanding of place. After becoming acquainted with the books of the Platonists, he writes, "I turned my gaze toward your invisible reality, trying to understand it through created things[.]" Although this approach did not provide Augustine with the understanding sought—for he was "rebuffed"—he "did perceive what that reality was which the darkness of my soul would not permit me to comtemplate. I was certain that you exist," and moreover "that you are infinite but not spread out through space either finite or infinite[.]"[91] Too, comes to Augustine appreciate the role of his own perception and cognition, which was one of the factors he had neglected earlier. Augustine reaches a realization

89. Augustine *Confessions* 7 (Boulding, 121).
90. Ibid.
91. Ibid.

Patristic Precedents

about the content of what he perceives, which are not (as he had thought) material forms but images. Augustine had previously believed that, since he believed himself to be seeing material things, that reality was extended. Shifting his understanding, Augustine comes to appreciate the role his mind played in generating mental representations, which are not material.

The possibilities thus opened up for Augustine are manifold, and reveal a more sophisticated understanding of the intersection of place and epistemology. Augustine comes to appreciate the possibility of non-corporeal realities, intelligible realities, which he is able to perceive not through the sense perception of his eyes but by his mind, in the immaterial light of truth itself, which is God.[92] In other words, God bestows that by which things are true—that, for example, by which Augustine's mental representation of created being can be a *true* representation of a created being. It is this illuminating role of God that Augustine had previously missed, when he too closely and too simply identified the contents of his visual field with reality itself. Hand in hand with his newfound understanding that God is the light of truth, come other realizations: that God is the source of all Being; that God's incorporeality does not mean that God is nothing; that God is not able to be divided (which had been his worry); and that all creatures exist through participation in God who bestows being. As Ayres suggests, this shift may constitute Augustine's most important shift in theological understanding and in any even remained with him until his death.[93] From this point forward, Augustine understands that God's omnipresence conditions materiality and extension, rather than the other way around.[94] Divine simplicity, though not specifically treated in this passage, was already assumed—for it was on the basis of divine simplicity that Augustine had first found fault with the notion of God as infinite extension. Accordingly, divine simplicity is (in Ayres' words) "treated as an essential corollary of . . . God as immaterial, unchangeable, and as Truth itself."[95]

In this way Augustine positions his own conception of God relative to two rival notions: that of the Manicheans, and that of Neo-Platonist philosophy. The Manicheans devalued the cosmos by dreaming up mendacious fables in which the cosmos became an arena for the hostile struggle between light and darkness. Augustine took particular offense at this notion, not

92. Ibid., 10.
93. Ayres, *Nicaea and Its Legacy*, 366–67.
94. St. Augustine, *The Confessions*, 189. See also Ayres, *Nicaea and Its Legacy*, 366–67.
95. Ayres, *Nicaea and Its Legacy*, 367.

The Place of the Spirit

only because it presumed to plot God according to spatial extension, but because it also devalued the cosmos in which the true God takes pleasure.[96] Philosophy, by contrast, does yield truths about the cosmos and God; it can suggest, for example, a notion of divine omnipresence which does not coincide with infinite spatial extension. The idolatrous turn comes when the philosophers attribute their discoveries to their own cleverness, without asking how it was that they came to have the ability to perceive truth in the first place.[97] As Augustine portrays it, there is a deep sympathy between such philosophical hubris, and the idea that the cosmos emanated by necessity. Both claims reveal a presumed entitlement to Truth and Being—a presumption that one can lay claim to them, make them work according to the same logic and schedule and parameters by which one's own mind works. In fact, though, human intellects can lay no such claim to truth and being. They are neither things we exist alongside, nor fellow instances in an overarching process of cosmic emanation from the One, nor discrete items which our intellects can receive impressions from and store in memory. God, the source of being and truth, is the one by whom we exist; the one by whose word the cosmos was made; and the truth whereby our own intellects may notice and apprehend true impressions of things as they are imprinted in memory.

This is all worked out along trinitarian lines, and can be understood as being worked out along placial lines as well—if we are willing to import a somewhat anachronistic notion of place. For the most pertinent passages do not always turn out to be those in which Augustine thematizes space or location. Rather, similar to the Cappadocians, it is the human activities of seeing and knowing—and the way in which these bear upon seeking the God who created us and seeks us—which best serve to link trinity and place. Part of Augustine's theological artistry lies, it seems to me, in how he plays different kinds of interiority and exteriority off each other, so as to effect a very particular change in perspective. Please note that I am meaning to use interiority and exteriority as my own, rather anachronistic shorthand here—my own grouping of concepts, metaphors, examples, and argumentative moves in Augustine's work that I see as being of a piece. This is very different from saying that Augustine has a particular understanding

---

96. Augustine *Confessions* (Boulding, 30); Also Miller, "Idolatry and the Polemics of World-Formation from Philo to Augustine," 139.

97. Miller, "Idolatry and the Polemics of World-Formation from Philo to Augustine," 144.

of interiority as such.[98] I include, for example, Augustine's language of mission, carrying as it does a connotation of some sort of purposeful traversal into creation, from the outside to its interior. I mean also to include the sense in which a mental representation of a thing is manufactured out of sense perceptions and put into the nonphysical space of the mind. I also include Augustine's notion that the time of creation is in the Word, timelessly, that the pre-incarnate Word is in creation, and, further, Augustine's juxtaposition of "inner spiritual things" and "outer bodily things," with the latter being those realities to which "our interest slips back and throws itself . . . in such a strangely persistent manner[.]"[99]

All of these have to do with whether and how we can know, and know God. Much like the Cappadocians, the perspective Augustine hopes to change is the perspective of one who presumes authoritatively to survey everything in one's own sight without once inquiring how one got the ability to see or to comprehend, let alone loving the one from whom the ability comes. If the shift is successful, one comes to see this ability—the ability to navigate the world of things, signs, referents—as itself contingent, known by and referring to another. There are any number of ways one might represent this truth to oneself. Perhaps one might locate and expound upon *vestigia* in our cognitive processes themselves, thus cobbling together a derivative mental representation of how God can be simple yet also triune. Perhaps not; and if the mental representations fail to persuade, it does not follow that the trinity is disproven. Alternatively, we might do what Augustine suggests in *De Trinitate* VII: consider all the things we love that are good, and then "[t]ake away this and that and see only good itself if you can."[100] In any event, we are not without mental resources or powers—but those powers tend persistently to what they are accustomed to working with: discrete, divisible, physical, bodies. Building a case for the trinity that takes its starting point from the set of items we normally deal

---

98. I certainly do not wish to suggest that Augustine invents inner subjective depths of the sort that moderns understand ourselves to have. On this point I disagree with Phillip Cary's position in Cary, *Augustine's Invention of the Inner Self*, since I am persuaded by the countervailing argument laid forth in, e.g., Cavadini's review in *Modern Theology*: "Nor does Augustine use the phrase 'private inner space', and this is not simply prevarication. 'Space' is a more generalized, concept-like word, which has the effect of literalizing the fleeting use of 'interior place' by Augustine, a phrase Augustine almost always uses in passages meant largely to point out its limitations" (428).

99. Augustine, *Trinity*, 303.

100. Ibid., 243–44.

with—quantifiable, locatable, time-bound entities—may be prudent under certain circumstances, but it hardly comes without dangers, chief among which is that we might end up loving the wrong thing. It would be all too easy, Augustine constantly warns, to love the mental representation of triunity which we are clever enough to come up with—or, perhaps, the mental faculties that allow us to manufacture such representations.

And so Augustine inserts strategic dodges, provisos, and qualifiers. I follow Benner in noting as significant the fact that Augustine begins *De Trinitate* with what he offers as scriptural evidence for a co-equal trinity of persons; if Augustine is truly arguing from the priority of divine essence, as is sometimes alleged, then this preoccupation was not reflected in the structuring of the text. Tellingly as well, Augustine also begins of Book V— *after* his discussion of scripture and the economy, and before his discussion of the divine essence, divine simplicity, and the mental image—that "[f]rom now on I will be attempting to say things that cannot altogether be said as they are thought by a man[,]" since "when we think about God the trinity we are aware that our thoughts are quite inadequate to their object[.]"[101] I see metaphors of inside and outside serving much the same end. "Here" and "there" are *not* straightforward or fixed when it comes to the triune God in creation. Rather, inside and outside behave in oblique, aslant ways, themselves becoming questioned in the process. Self-enclosed preconstituted domains—whether of subjectivity, creatureliness, the mind, or divinity—are appealed to, certainly; but they are also subverted, exactly because those domains are the way in which our minds ordinarily categorize things.

For this reason, their operation turns out to be tremendously complicated. We apprehend truths of outside things by representing them in our intellects; we can see truths in creation; we can navigate within the cosmos and, in our temporally distended way, come up with true insights through the interior activity of navigating within memory. We can even use such mental processes as a way of imagining how triunity might work. But qualification upon qualification follows. We err terribly if we think that God is in the cosmos in a physically extended way, as discussed earlier. We err as well if we notice our ability to navigate the world of things and signs, and thereby conclude that it refers *ultimately* to an inner faculty of reasoning. To the contrary, that ability to reason—to see, navigate, and comprehend—comes from outside ourselves. God is the light by which

101. Ibid., 189.

we are able to see truth, navigate within the memory, and structure and participate in the world (one might even say built environment) of words and signs and things. Moreover, creation is in God the Word, even as God the Word is in creation; all the moments of creation are in the Word before time—while meanwhile the Word is present in creation even before the time of the incarnation, ultimately reaching the fullness of time which was already contained in the Word itself.[102]

Finally, there are the processions and missions of the Father, Son, and Spirit: the way in which all three persons share the one essence and work in concert, but differ according to procession (outside of time) and mission (within time). The Son is different from the Father because the Son is begotten of the Father; but this difference has to do with the Son's procession, not the Son's essence. The Spirit, likewise, shares in the divine essence while also having its own relationship of procession; and famously, the Spirit shows up as the "donum" or "caritas" between Father and Son. The emphasis given divine essence, and the Spirit's status as gift or bond, are moves for which Augustine is often criticized. Critics allege that these aspects of Augustine's thought tend to reduce, depersonalize, or subordinate the Spirit, and perhaps collapse the entire trinity into a monad. While I appreciate the criticisms, I think that these are two points which can be most fruitfully reworked into a trinitarian theology of place.

It may help to consider, again, what is at stake for Augustine in the doctrine of divine simplicity. If God is not simple, then the only way available for God to be everywhere present, is to be everywhere spatially extended and distended. As discussed, Augustine is concerned that such a quantity could be divided up into physical parts or temporal moments. Such a divisible and distended quantity could not function as that by which all true and intelligible things are true and intelligible. If this seems to press against triunity, it is only because of our "flesh-bound habit of thought" which "perceives [only] as far as its powers extend."[103] It would be overreaching, I think, to surmise that Augustine's only reason for emphasizing the shared divine essence is in order to safeguard divine simplicity. However, I am here trying to reappropriate Augustine's trinitarian theology in service of a theology of place which is both trinitarian, and which accounts for contemporary reflection on place. To this end, it is worth noticing how divine simplicity and divine essence operate, for Augustine, in concert.

102. Ibid., 230–32.
103. Ibid., 242.

The Place of the Spirit

Both have to do with a kind of presence which does not entail divisibility; and divisibility, in turn, evokes the sort of quantity that is spread out in space—the very sort of quantity we can straightforwardly see and represent with the "flesh-bound habit of thought." Seeing as how this latter outcome is exactly what Augustine hopes to avoid, then what can one say about the Spirit as the love or bond between the Father and Son? One can hardly say that this "between" is a straightforward interval, if one wishes to be true to Augustine.

In conclusion, as we move now into a discussion of two contemporary figures, I think it is worth bearing in mind the way in which fourth and early fifth century trinitarian thought gives placial cues, even if place is not defined in the same way as it will be in the late modern project of placial advocacy. If one is willing, in one's survey of the thinkers treated in this chapter, to treat metaphors as suggestive of that theologian's placial sensibilities, one finds much richness and depth. As I shall argue in chapter five, that constitutes one possible point of connection between patristic theology and late modern placial advocacy. More broadly, though, these theologians' attention to the structures of human knowledge—and the ways in which human knowledge involves place-freighted and space-freighted activities like delimitation and location—is instructive. In the course of this discussion, admittedly, they do not tend to treat place as a sub-topic within epistemology. Nevertheless, their considerations of creaturely perspective are very useful, given all they accomplish. All four of these theologians—perhaps Basil and Augustine in particular—link human perspectival knowing to triunity without collapsing the trinity into human perspectives. Relatedly, all describe the possibility of knowledge about God (and even to varying degrees natural theology) without requiring that God satisfy human conceptual specifications. These issues, to put it mildly do not get laid to rest in contemporary trinitarian thought. Indeed, as we shall see in the next two chapters, the stakes are raised.

3

Moltmann's Perichoretic Spaces for God and Creation

Changed Stakes

As the patristic interlocutors exit the stage for a moment, we are (I hope) left feeling somewhat optimistic about the possibility of a trinitarian theology of place. To be sure, some theological disclaimers are needed as a raised warning flag to remind passersby that although place may be grounded in trinitarian activity, human-made conceptions are ultimately finite; it cannot be that the trinity is subsumed to place.

Moving to the two contemporary theologians, we find the stakes changed somewhat. The difference is difficult to perceive at first. For here, as in the fourth century, trinitarian models, understandings of place, and theological epistemology exercise mutual influence upon each other. Certain elements, certain ways in which the influence is exercised, are left implicit but they can be teased out. Provisionally, I suggest that one notable difference is that theologically-fraught created arenas for God's activity—arenas into which one is trying to put God; or out of which one is trying to get God—are a bit more explicitly spatialized. This may seem a counterintuitive suggestion. After all, my patristic interlocutors—when they thematized place or space—tended to equate it with corporeal extension. With the patristic authors, though, there were hints of a placial retrieval: a way in which place and space ended up having a trinitarian grounding, without the trinity ever being conditioned by place or space. Moltmann and Marion also attempt placial retrievals, but they play out differently. My best explanation for this discrepancy is that the stakes have changed.

The Place of the Spirit

Now, place and space signal nothing so much as the created horizon posed as theological problem: placial and spatial images indicate that in which God needs to be and act in order to be here with us (Moltmann); or else placial language indicates that in which one *cannot* put God lest one lapse into idolatry (Marion). The solution afforded by Nyssen's boundary—the "middle wall" which marks creation's limit with respect to God, but not the reverse—is therefore muted. This change exercises trinitarian influence, too, because for both theologians the trinity is pressed into the service of this particular theological problem. The notion of God showing up within a horizon is now considered a problem for Christian theology which the doctrine of the trinity has been recruited to help solve.

Turning, then, to Moltmann. One welcome characteristic of Moltmann's work, for the purposes of the present inquiry, is that he does—in his later writing—attend to place explicitly. This turn to place takes place later in his career—sounding with particular fullness in *God in Creation*—after he has spent decades as a theologian of history. Too, in his 2000 book on theological method, *Experiences in Theology: Ways and Forms of Christian Theology*, Moltmann suggests connections between his more recent work on place, and his theological epistemology. In teasing out Moltmann's developing theology of place, an important task will therefore be to attend closely to the other developments in his theology that propel him toward this consideration of place. To anticipate and flag my conclusion in advance: what Moltmann reveals about place and epistemology in *Experiences* is, I think, indicated all along—in his more recent turn to place, but also in his previous work in which place is not treated as explicitly.

For in his early trilogy—*Theology of Hope, The Crucified God*, and *The Church in the Power of the Spirit*—Moltmann is primarily dealing with the historical (rather than spatial or placial) horizon in which God is confessed to act. History, as Moltmann uses the category, assumes that human meaning making happens because we understand ourselves to be moving toward something... while meanwhile drawing on the communities and understandings that have preceded us. Likewise "hope"—arguably Moltmann's central theological concept in this early work—names the redemptive, transformed possibility of human history when God acts within its bounds. In so doing, the early Moltmann challenges certain eschatological, soteriological, and ecclesiological impulses in Christian theology which he believes possess an anemic understanding of history. Though he does not treat place, it is easy to see how the most pared-down version of Moltmann's thesis about history—i.e. that humans inhabit a certain horizon, and that God is at work within that horizon to bring it toward its ultimate fulfillment—suggest certain possibilities for place.

But that is, as I say, the early Moltmann. Moltmann makes an important shift after the early trilogy, beginning with *Trinity and the Kingdom of God*. There, motivated in part by the critical reception of *Theology of Hope*, Moltmann considers the relationship of the three divine persons to each other. We must note well the nature of the criticism leveled at the early trilogy. Many readers of Moltmann had detected, in his early work, a Hegelian undertow which tended to make God's action and human history two respective moments within one overarching process.[1] Moltmann's response, in *Trinity and the Kingdom*, is to rearrange some major elements of his theology, such that the "history of the Trinity" (and what this means shall of course need to be explored) more clearly situates human history, without being flatly conditioned by it. He thereby lessens the appearance that both histories are moments within some more all-encompassing horizon of God's self-realization.

This approach, as I see it, carries him through the 1980s and 1990s, and it is at that point that Moltmann begins a sustained theological consideration of place. But then, in *God in Creation* and *The Coming of God*, Moltmann begins thinking about how place and space may be defined theologically; and even more fundamentally, how space (like history) is a horizon in which God and people dwell and act. (His interests here arise in the context of his growing interest in ecology during these years, as well as his interest in theology's intersection with science.) In crafting an understanding of place and space, Moltmann re-uses the conceptual machinery from his earlier work, when he had so focused on history as the horizon for God's action. Thus, he is explicitly critical of the domain of "absolute space," punctuate and uniform, passive and viewed objectively. Indeed, Moltmann

---

1. Not all who noted the Hegelian structure were critical; some of Moltmann's most thorough readers merely note the influence. See, for example, Meeks' discussion in *Origins of the Theology of Hope*, where he notes that "Moltmann often works with the Hegelian insight learned from Iwand that the subject and object cannot be totally separated even in faith's knowledge of God" (39). See also Bauckham's later and more retrospective work, *Theology of Jürgen Moltmann*, in which he notes that the early Moltmann—in distinction to Ernst Bloch—believes that hope requires divine transcendence in order to overcome an absolute negative which Moltmann quite clearly views in Hegelian terms (44). McDougall discusses the critical appraisal—whether merely noted or leveled as an accusation—that *Theology of Hope* was heavily Hegelian in structure. See chapter 3 of *Pilgrimage of Divine Love*.

The Place of the Spirit

unleashes a sustained critique of absolute space in *God in Creation*, in a section entitled "Creation of Spaces and Space of Creation," about which I shall say more in a moment. Suffice it to say, for now, that this is Moltmann at his most Bachelardian. True to his earlier work on history, Moltmann is interested in life, in dwelling. Later in *God in Creation* Moltmann takes a term with predominantly temporal significance—Sabbath—and reworks it placially, stating that "God does not merely 'rest from' his works, or rest only in the face of his works. He also rests *in* his works. He allows them to exist in his presence."[2] These are all useful insights, fruitful insofar as they render explicit the connection between place and doctrine of God, by way of a doctrine of creation.

The only criticism I note—as one interested in using these elements Moltmann's thought to inform a trinitarian theology of place—is the unease with which these elements rest alongside Moltmann's dialectical moments. For Moltmann remains committed to a dialectical structure, even when his aim is to give this structure a trinitarian grounding. As I read Moltmann, his dialectical structure tends to reach for domains, perhaps in spite of his placial interests. Indeed, to some degree, Moltmann indicates as much in the title of his most placial work *God in Creation*. There are two different realities—God, and creation—that are meant to co-inhere each other. They function, in a sense, as domains. To be sure, for Moltmann, domains (like systems, horizons, and indeed history) can be open or closed, and accordingly Moltmann posits a mutual openness between God and creation. Nevertheless, the undertow persists; places have a kind of expansiveness to them that is prior and somewhat self-constituting, though they realize themselves in a coinherence with the other. Indeed, Moltmann's designation as a panentheist suggests this notion of place writ large; God and the world coinhere each other, bridging the gulf between each other, making each other's places their own.

Accordingly, the features of place that have to do with perspectival world-structuring tend to drop out of these parts of Moltmann's theology. This is indicated all along, but finally becomes explicit in *Experiences in Theology*, Moltmann's book on theological method. There he goes through many different models for knowing God, stating a preference for and consequently advocating a dialectical model. A dialectical model of human knowing makes sense, given the other dialectical elements of Moltmann's

---

2. Moltmann, *God in Creation*, 279.

thought. However, such a model serves to mute the (in my opinion) most promising elements of Moltmann's placial thought.

There is another tension—possibly subsidiary to the one just mentioned—that I also detect in Moltmann's later work on place. Sometimes Moltmann seems to adopt an understanding of place wherein one quantity or entity must withdraw, depart, or self-restrict in order to make room for another. At other times, Moltmann invokes the non-restrictive language of perichoresis to talk about the placing of God and creation, and the three persons with respect to each other. So is God, as triune, placed in a perichoretic fashion—in contrast to creation's being located by means of limit and restriction? Or are both God and creation placed according to the restrictive definition, since it is God's own self-restriction that first throws open primordial space? Or are there ways in place is both restrictive and perichoretic—whether the placed quantity is God or creation? As I read Moltmann, he is somewhat unclear.

This, at any rate, is the critique I intend to offer in the present chapter. I shall first look at Moltmann's breakthrough work, *Theology of Hope*. My intention is not to downplay the importance of *The Crucified God* or *The Church in the Power of the Spirit*. Neither work is simply a rehashing of *Theology of Hope*, and *The Crucified God* in particular contains some important fleshing-out of Christ's saving work on the cross.[3] Nevertheless, the elements that influence Moltmann's later treatment of place are mostly consistent throughout the three books of the early trilogy, and are most clearly laid out in *Theology of Hope*. The differences in focus and emphasis between *Theology of Hope* and *The Crucified God*, and again between *The Crucified God* and *The Church in the Power of the Spirit*, though important, are for the most part not central to the tensions in Moltmann's later work on place. The differences between *Theology of Hope* and *Trinity and the Kingdom*, on the other hand, are of paramount importance for Moltmann's theology of place, so I shall spend some time looking at *Trinity and the Kingdom* in depth. I shall then look at Moltmann's discussions of place in *God in Creation* and *The Coming of God*, and finally close with a brief look at *Experiences in Theology*, where many of the assumptions indicated all along become explicit.

---

3. For a summary, see Bauckham, *Theology of Jürgen Moltmann*, 47–69.

History as Horizon in Theology of Hope

"God is not somewhere in the Beyond, but he is coming and as the coming One he is present."[4] With these words from *Theology of Hope,* Moltmann condenses the most important elements of his early work into a succinct description of God as one in whom presence and futurity coincide. With these same words Moltmann also displays his distaste for any Christian theology that places too much stock in a "Beyond," a horizon different from the historical horizon in which Christians await the coming God. These two concerns constitute framing themes in Moltmann's early work. To understand why these two concerns assume such central importance, we must take into account his interlocutors. As McDougall, Bauckham, and Meeks all point out, Moltmann's work during this period has as its pastoral concern the recovery of a sense of eschatological hope and urgency in Christian theology.[5] Any discussion of Moltmann as a "dialectical theologian" must bear this in mind. For in fact Moltmann is engaged in sustained criticism of the *previous* generation of dialectical theologians, Barth and Bultmann in particular. Specifically, Moltmann is vexed by what he sees as their tendency to "make . . . the *eschaton* into a transcendental eternity, the transcendental meaning of all ages, equally near to all the ages of history and equally far from all of them."[6]

If this is what eschatology is, asks Moltmann, then on what possible basis should Christians have eschatological hope while still living in history? That is, if eschatological fulfillment lies squarely on the other side of a static rupture between temporality and eternity—if it is not advancing, but is equally distant and equally close to this and every other historical moment—then what do Christians, particularly those who suffer, await? And what basis does this dehistoricized eschatology have in scripture, with

---

4. Moltmann, *Theology of Hope,* 164.

5. Bauckham, *Theology of Jürgen Moltmann,* 30: "Pannenberg, Moltmann and others saw in future eschatology precisely the way to make Christian faith credible and relevant in the modern world." Meeks, *Origins of the Theology of Hope,* 4–5: "The prevailing theologies of the later forties and fifties . . . were peculiarly ineffective in showing the 'unseasonable,' critical nature of the Christian message for the present culture. Nor were they able to show how Christian faith is related to the real determination of human history." McDougall, *Pilgrimage of Love,* 31: "Of special concern to Moltmann were the damaging social and political consequences concern to Moltmann were the damaging social and political consequences that these dehistoricized models of eschatology held for contemporary Christianity."

6. Moltmann, *Theology of Hope,* 39–40.

its many appeals to the quickly approaching day of the Lord, and with its apocalyptic horizon?[7] Moltmann's aim in *Theology of Hope* is to recover an eschatological hope that he believes has lately been obscured, by means of a theological reorientation that makes God's promise-fulfillment a decidedly historical, decidedly future-oriented reality.

It is at this point, in most overviews of Moltmann's thought, that a commentator is likely to introduce Ernst Bloch and his role (and through him, Hegel's role) on Moltmann's thought; and, having done so, discuss whether and how Moltmann is a dialectical theologian in a same or different vein as Bloch or Hegel. Certainly any thorough discussion of Moltmann and dialectic cannot leave this discussion out entirely. I propose, though, to postpone that discussion for a moment, and focus a bit more closely on promise fulfillment, a theme Moltmann returns to again and again, importantly, in his discussions of who God is. This gets at a crucial aspect of Moltmann's early theology—but one that it is all too easy to miss if one rushes to a discussion of Bloch and Hegel. Even in his early work, Moltmann moves with ease from epistemology to theology—from discussions of the availability of God's self-revelation to historically bound human knowers, to discussions of who God is. Why is this startling? Simply because it is one thing to say that God is who God reveals godself to be in history; and quite another to say that if history conditions God's self-revelation, then God is one who is conditioned by history. And the latter does indeed seem to be what Moltmann is saying, with his focus on promise-fulfillment.

Viewed in this light, the sections of *Theology of Hope* that contain lengthy summations of God's acts in salvation history—the Abrahamic promise and its fulfillment, the messianic promise and its fulfillment[8]—lay the groundwork for a claim Moltmann makes about revelation and the knowability of God. God is only known, Moltmann points out, through the promises God has made and fulfilled to God's people, in history. If the knowledge thus gained reflects the true self-revelation of God, Moltmann reasons, then it follows that God is identifiable as the one who acts thus in history. In Moltmann's words, "God reveals himself as 'God' where he shows himself as the same and is thus known as the same. He becomes identifiable where he identifies himself with himself in the historic act of his faithfulness."[9] Elsewhere, even more explicitly, Moltmann states,

7. McDougall, *Pilgrimage of Love*, 31–32.
8. Moltmann, *Theology of Hope*, 106.
9. Ibid., 116.

"[I]n the New Testament God is known and described as the 'God of promise'. . . . His essence is not his absoluteness as such, but the faithfulness with which he reveals and identifies himself in the history of his promise as 'the same.'"[10] God's essence, God's very identity, consists in the faithfulness with which God fulfills God's promises in history—for this is the God who has been revealed.

Of course at this point the burning question is, does this historical faithfulness pick out God without remainder? Is there anything left of God that isn't found within a historical horizon? By way of an answer, let us recall the quotation with which I began this section: God is "coming and as the coming One he is present."[11] The stipulation that God is coming *into* history *from* its eschatological end is, precisely, as much of remainder as Moltmann will allow, no more and no less. But it is important to notice that even this remainder is not something other than God's presence in history as the coming One. To the contrary, God's presence in history as the one who is coming, is what gives history its future-orientation. Although God's promises have been fulfilled—Abraham's descendants have become a landed people, the messiah did come—this very fulfillment points beyond itself to the eschatological fulfillment that is still ahead, at the end of history. Put differently, these historical fulfillments contain, in Moltmann's words, an "overspill that points to the future[.]"[12] The "overspill" and what I have been calling the remainder turn out to be one and the same, exactly because God's self-revelation in history and God's identity (as the One who is coming) are the same.

The point I am working my way around to is this: in Moltmann's early work, this particular understanding of revelation provides the soil in which his cuttings from Hegel and Bloch take root. It is not simply that Moltmann ends up with a dialectical streak because he is indebted to Bloch and therefore to Hegel. Rather, Moltmann finds Bloch amenable because he, like Bloch, saw biblical narrative—and the messianic promise in particular—as a powerful source of hope in history, and as a motivator for the transformation of social and political institutions. But where Bloch wished to uproot this hope from its religious medium and re-plant it in a demythologized humanism,[13] Moltmann believes that salvation history testifies to—and in

10. Ibid., 143.
11. Ibid., 164.
12. Ibid., 109.
13. McDougall, *Pilgrimage of Love*, 34–35.

some profound sense, *gives us*—the God who is coming from history's end *for the purpose of* fulfilling God's promises by conquering godforsakenness and death.

And this is where dialectic enters the picture. Moltmann has so far taken every opportunity to trouble any distinctions between 1) who God is revealed to be in history, 2) who God will be revealed to be at history's eschatological end, and 3) who God is in godself. I have suggested already that Moltmann's interests here include preserving Christian hope, giving theological meaning to history, and affirming the trustworthiness of historical revelation. To these I now add another. For Moltmann, it seems, the self-identity of God is at stake—and with the self-identity of God, our future hope. For Moltmann is here concerned with the contraries of (in McDougall's words) "absence and presence, suffering and hope, hell and bliss.[14] Moltmann's assertion is that only God's self-identity can bear these seemingly unbearable contraries—and in so doing, bring presence from absence, hope from suffering, bliss from hell, life from death, creation from nothing.

We see this particularly clearly in Moltmann's discussion of cross and resurrection. Moltmann emphasizes that in the post-resurrection appearances, the resurrected, living, glorified Christ speaks words that express his personal identity with the crucified, dead, godforsaken Christ. As Moltmann explains, "[w]ithout words spoken and heard the Easter appearances would have remained ghostly things . . . hierophanies of a new, divine spiritual Being." Instead, Jesus speaks "something in the nature of a self-identification ('It is I')" and that self-identity entails "continuity in radical discontinuity, or an identity in total contradiction."[15] Godforsakenness and glorification, promise and fulfillment, present suffering and coming bliss—these contradictions are held in identity in "the identity of Jesus," which in turn "can be understood only as an identity *in*, but not above and beyond, cross and resurrection."[16] The nature of the aforementioned overspill, then, is revealed in this dialectic of cross and resurrection. Whatever allows the crucified Jesus and the resurrected Jesus to share the property of identity, must be an "event in between . . . an eschatological event . . . a new totality which annihilates the total *nihil*" of godforsakenness to which Christ, the God-man, had succumbed on the cross. Happening as it does in the middle

14. Ibid., 30.
15. Moltmann, *Theology of Hope*, 198–99.
16. Ibid., 199.

of history, this event "has set in motion an eschatologically determined process of history, whose goal . . ."—proleptically here already in Christ—". . . is the annihilation of death in the victory of the life of the resurrection"[17] In other words, in the resurrection we see history opening up, transcending itself, to contains something that is *not* history: eschatological fulfillment. In one and the same motion, however, this very revelation of eschatological fulfillment is a case of the promised future transcending itself—breaking in upon history from its end, catching all of the negativities and nihils, and bringing them within an eschatological horizon that actually *gives* history its end.

At this point I believe we have flagged most of the elements of *Theology of Hope* that will be important for understanding (and, at points, taking issue with) Moltmann's later theological reflections on place. Perhaps the best way to sum up our discussion is by asking, does the Moltmann of *Theology of Hope* envision a dialectical movement of divine self-explication on the one hand, and finite self-transcendence on the other—with the latter occurring as a moment in the former? Put differently (and echoing some of the criticisms of *Theology of Hope*) does Moltmann have God becoming God through God's acts in history? Or even more pointedly, do we see in Moltmann just warned-over German Idealism a la Hegel or baptized Marxism a la Bloch? At the very least, it seems clear that Moltmann has deliberately included hedges against his conclusion: the "overspill" that points to God's futurity, the eschatological horizon for revelation, the insistence that God gives history its end. These hedges do, I think, mitigate against the conclusion that God is exhaustively subject to the historical horizon in every sense. And yet, there are hedges against the hedges. Moltmann repeatedly insists that God *is* who God has revealed godself to be in history, and is impatient with any further distinction between God's historical revelation and God *in se*. Moreover, God has revealed godself to be precisely the Coming One, whose coming will bring life out of death and blessedness out of godforsakenness. From this angle, it does seem as though God needs the nihils and negativities of history in order for God's self-revelation—which, again, is not something other than God's very identity—to occur.

17. Ibid., 163.

The History of God in Trinity and the Kingdom

Moltmann himself understood *Trinity and the Kingdom* to represent a turning point in his work. In the late 1970's—following the publication of *Theology of Hope, The Crucified God*, and *The Church in the Power of the Spirit*—Moltmann had set as his goal a major work on the trinity that would "integrate all of the historical experiences and therefore speak of the [trinitarian] persons, their relations and the changes in their relationships, i.e., of their history."[18] This integration would be given in a new systematic form—what he first called a "messianic Dogmatics,"[19] but later changed to "systematic contributions in theology," distinguishing this new project from the earlier works which "were programmatic in style and content."[20] *Trinity and the Kingdom* was the first of these systematic contributions, published in 1980.

Moltmann changed more than just his theological method. In response to the reception of his earlier work, Moltmann uses *Trinity and the Kingdom* as an attempt to clarify and amend aspects of *Theology of Hope* and *The Crucified God* that had appeared to equate the trinity with its history of relations to creation.[21] In *Theology of Hope,* as we have seen, Moltmann's thinking runs something like this: God's self-revelation to creation has occurred within the horizon of history, in which God has revealed godself as the fulfiller of promises. God's self-revelation is true. Therefore, God's very identity is realized in history through God's own promise-fulfillment. In *Trinity and the Kingdom,* by contrast, Moltmann's claims are more modest. To be sure, he still targets strains in Christian theology that he deems too static, too dehistoricized. But he approaches the issue differently. We might imagine Moltmann asking this question: Why would God create a historically bound humanity as the recipients of God's own self-revelation, only to require that those recipients then erase every hint of history from their understanding of who God statically is "in essence"? Isn't it far more likely that our historically conditioned existence actually primes us to understand something about who the triune God is in godself? In other words, isn't it likely that the relationships between the Father, Son, and Spirit will turn

---

18. Excerpted from Moltmann, "Antwort auf die Kritik an 'Der gekreutzigte Gott'" 186–87; translated by and cited in McDougall, *Pilgrimage of Love*, 68.
19. McDougall, *Pilgrimage of Love*, 68, n. 35.
20. Moltmann, *Trinity and the Kingdom*, xi
21. McDougall, *Pilgrimage of Love*, 19.

The Place of the Spirit

out to be something like a "trinitarian history"—a history grounding the created history that (it turns out) has faithfully corresponded to it all along?

Moltmann still takes issue with much of classical Christian reflection on the trinity, for he is disinclined to affirm that an a-pathetic God is the God attested to in Christian scripture. He therefore sets out to give a "trinitarian history," in which there is a relationship of correspondence between the trinitarian history of God and the self-revelation of God in history. Part of this trinitarian history involves moments of self-restriction and consequential letting-be—both on the part of the Father vis-à-vis the Son, and on the part of God vis-à-vis creation. Thus *Trinity and the Kingdom* begins with a frontal assault on what Moltmann sees to be two detrimental strands of western trinitarian thought—the substance model and the subject model—which Moltmann understands as having made trinitarian faith essentially unimportant to most western Christians.[22] As an exponent of the former, Moltmann cites the bulk of the Christian tradition since Tertullian, for whom, he says, "the Christian Trinity [is] . . . depicted as belonging within the general concept of the divine substance. . . . The one, indivisible, homogeneous divine substance is constituted as three individual, divine persons."[23] As an exponent of the latter, Moltmann offers Hegel, for whom the trinity is "represented in terms belonging to the general concept of the absolute subject: *one subject—three modes of being*."[24]

The problem, in both cases, is that God's unity—whether of substance or subject—is so emphasized, made so prior, rendered so foundational, that God's triunity ends up functioning as an add-on. In the case of the substance model, its shortcomings become clear when, in theology textbooks, there are two treatises on God: *De Deo uno* (in which it is assured that "there *is* a God and that God is *one*[,]") and *De Deo trino* (in which is given the special, revealed doctrine that this one God is in fact a *triune* God). In the case of the subject model, the unity is found in "the one, identical God-subject" whose reflection on itself yields three distinct self-communications: the "I," the "self," and the "I-self." Notably lacking from this philosophically tight picture, Moltmann points out, is anything resembling "the trinitarian concept of person, because the concept of person also contains the concept of the subject of acts and relationships[.]"[25]

22. Moltmann, *Trinity and the Kingdom*, 1.
23. Ibid., 16.
24. Ibid., 17.
25. Ibid., 17–18.

In place of these inadequate understandings of the trinitarian relations, Moltmann offers instead a "social doctrine of the Trinity," one which will proceed "in the light of . . . trinitarian history."[26] "Trinitarian history" is a new term, a new concept, one central to Moltmann's project in *Trinity and the Kingdom of God*. What tasks is it performing, in the context of Moltmann's overall argument? Certainly, "trinitarian history" reiterates Moltmann's earlier concern for history, for the historical nature of revelation and the historical horizon for the Christian life. In addition, "trinitarian history"—inasmuch as it connotes change—seals Moltmann's departure from the classical Christian doctrine of a God who does not change, react, undergo, or suffer. In fact Moltmann spends considerable time here rehearsing the criticisms he leveled in *Crucified God*, namely, that a God who is incapable of suffering in every respect is also incapable of love in every respect.[27] Both of these overarching aims help explain Moltmann's purpose in describing his trinitarian theology as a trinitarian history.

However, I believe we are mistaken if we understand "trinitarian history" only as a carry-over from Moltmann's earlier work. As I read Moltmann, "trinitarian history" exactly names the stipulation that Moltmann did *not* make—or at least, did not make clearly enough—in *Theology of Hope*. Specifically, by "trinitarian history," Moltmann has in mind something like what has more traditionally been called the immanent trinity. And here we note a sympathy between how Moltmann temporalizes both "kingdom" and the traditional (placially inflected) designation of the immanent trinity as "ad intra." "Kingdom," arguably a placial or at least geopolitical term, becomes temporalized in *Trinity and the Kingdom,* within three historical stages of human freedom respectively appropriated to Father,

26. Ibid., 19.

27. Ibid., 23. Bauckham criticizes Moltmann here for what he sees as an incautious transference between human definitions of personhood and trinitarian personhood, questioning whether Moltmann envisions a relationship of participation of human personhood in divine personhood, or rather a classification of both in terms of some overarching understanding of personhood: "Attractive as it is (and paralleled in the work of other contemporary theologians) there seem to me to be serious problems with this line of argument. Moltmann is trying to hold together the two rather different ideas: that (a) the life of the Trinity is an interpersonal fellowship in which we, by grace, participate, and (b) the life of the Trinity provides the prototype on which human life should be modeled . . . The two ideas would be fairly easily compatible were we to think of the Trinity as simply like a group of three friends who include us in their friendship as yet more friends . . . But it is misleading to think in that way of the Trinity and our participation in the life of the Trinity" (Bauckham, *Theology of Jürgen Moltmann*, 177).

Son, and Spirit.[28] Correspondingly, the relationships among Father, Son, and Spirit are explicated in the trinitarian history. As McDougall points out, Moltmann has contested—and continues to contest, in *Trinity and the Kingdom*—the traditional distinction between immanent and economic, based on his conviction that a self-contained, self-sufficient God of immanent relations is not the God who has been revealed in salvation history. Is there then no way to talk about who God is in godself, as unconditioned by God's relationship to the world? In *Theology of Hope*, as we have seen, Moltmann could be construed as answering no. In *Trinity and the Kingdom*, by contrast, Moltmann proposes a way to make claims about God *in se*: in the context of praise.[29] Believers, he suggests, initially praise God for God's grace and mercy toward humanity; but doxology eventually moves into praising God for God's own sake, simply because God is good. In this way, Moltmann tells us, what has traditionally been called the economic trinity is simply "the object of kerygmatic and practical theology; [while] the 'immanent Trinity' the content of doxological theology."[30]

Because there are not two different trinities, our doxological theology must be disciplined by the following principle: "we may not," Moltmann cautions, "assume anything as existing in God himself which contradicts the history of salvation; and, conversely, may not assume anything in the experience of salvation which does not have its foundation in God."[31] Within the context of doxology, in other words, we should expect to find a correspondence between God in the history of salvation, and God in godself. The trinitarian history, if I understand Moltmann correctly, names one party to this correspondence; while kingdom of God names the other. And Moltmann is emphatic that the trinitarian history must indeed have a historical structure, with something akin to distinguishable subjects, actions, and moments. Otherwise it would precisely *not* cohere with the history of salvation, in which the Father, Son, and Spirit perform different works at different moments.

So what is this trinitarian history, expounded in the context of doxology, and corresponding to salvation history? Earlier I mentioned Moltmann's use of the 1 John formulation, "God is love," in his defense of the claim that God suffers. As it turns out, Moltmann's trinitarian history is an

28. Bauckham, *Theology of Jürgen Moltmann*, 180ff.
29. McDougall, *Pilgrimage of Love*, 91.
30. Moltmann, *Trinity and the Kingdom*, 152.
31. Ibid.

extended meditation upon this verse—and, consequently, upon a God who, as love, is *"the self-communication of the good . . . the power of good to go out of itself, to enter into other being, to participate in other being, and to give itself to other being[.]"*[32] Further, if God is indeed love, Moltmann avers, then God must be understood as triune; for "Love cannot be consumed by a solitary subject . . . If God is love he is at once the lover, the beloved and the love itself."[33] The Father, as lover, engenders and brings forth the Son in eternity; the Son, as beloved, responds to the Father's love in obedience and surrender; and the Spirit, as the love, is the self-communicating goodness by virtue of which the Father begets the Son.[34]

To stop here—compelling though this picture may be—is to risk obscuring Moltmann's entire point (as well as miss the implications for Moltmann's later work on place). The eternal trinitarian self-differentiation of the God who is Love is, Moltmann tells us, necessary and not free. By contrast, God's bringing forth a creation out of nothing is free, though "axiomatic." What should one make of these distinctions? What hangs on them? Here again, I understand Moltmann to be making the point that had arguably been obscured in his earlier work, namely that God does not need creation in order to be God. Here, God is under no *external* compulsion to create, but it is worth noting that the contrast Moltmann draws is between the "necessary" outcome of the trinitarian relations, and the "axiomatic" outcome of creation. As discussed already, if God is indeed Love, then for Moltmann it is logically necessary that God will be triune. For love is precisely the self-communication of the good, and this self-communication in turn requires a threefold self-differentiation. Considered under the aspect of the immanent trinity, the love between the Father, Son, and Spirit is therefore necessary. By contrast, it is "axiomatic" that a God who is love will *freely* create and *freely* love a free Other. "Axiomatic," in this sense, means only that God "cannot deny himself" by not loving freely.[35] God loves freely, not because God is under compulsion to do so, but because God is God; and God's freedom is precisely "his vulnerable love, his openness, the encountering kindness through which he suffers with the human beings he loves and becomes their advocate[.]"[36]

32. Ibid., 57, italics in original.
33. Ibid.
34. Ibid., 59.
35. Ibid., 107.
36. Ibid., 56.

The Place of the Spirit

And here, at long last, we have worked our way to Moltmann's idea of God's inward self-restriction—which, for Moltmann, follows on the heels of God's free and creative love. "With the creation of a world which is not God, but which none the less corresponds to him," Moltmann explains, "*God's self-humiliation* begins—the self-limitation of the One who is omnipresent, and the suffering of eternal love." Again, we see Moltmann stressing the correspondence of the world to the trinitarian history of God; but now, it seems, this correspondence coincides with God freely suffering a self-imposed limitation. It is a self-limitation, because "the Creator has to concede to his creation the space in which it can exist. He must take time for that creation, and allow it time."[37] And it is suffering, because God "it is . . . 'an act of God inwardly', which means that it is something that God suffers and endures."[38]

Some observations are in order. First, it is worth noting that the problem Moltmann appears to be solving here—the problem of how there can be room for creation in the first place—could not have shown up in *Theology of Hope*. That is to say, the problem is itself a function of the new laws of theological physics that Moltmann has put into play in *Trinity and the Kingdom*, according to which one may discern a God who is self-communicating love *in se*. For in that case the question does indeed arise, "How does there come to be room for God's Other in the first place? Does not the eternal self-differentiation of Father, Son, and Spirit exhaust all possibilities for relation?" But this question would lose all its urgency, and indeed its coherence, should one try to couch it in the terms of *Theology of Hope*. There, we recall, God was defined as "the coming One who is present" in history, and in whose identity life comes from death, presence from absence, redemption from godforsakenness. Far from crowding out a free creation, Moltmann's earlier definition of God seems to require it.

Second, as mentioned above, the force of the problem depends upon a restrictive definition of place, at least in the sense that God's presence and creation's room are quantities wherein one must be restricted to make room for the other. We shall see, this writ large, later in *The Coming of God*.

Third, the divine self-restriction is said here to have taken place inwardly. God in godself is the subject of the self-limiting action; it is for this reason that the self-limitation is said to be suffered and endured by God. Yet Moltmann has also said that the divine self-limitation begins

---

37. Ibid., 59.
38. Ibid.

"[w]ith the creation of a world which is not God, but which none the less corresponds to him." How does this square with the Moltmann's own rules governing doxological theology? We recall that, for Moltmann, doxology moves from praising God for God's saving acts, to praising God because God is good *in se*. For this reason, Moltmann will grant a certain legitimacy to theological discussions of the immanent trinity—provided they are understood doxologically. In light of that, how can Moltmann now say that this self-limitation is an "act of God inwardly," *and* that it occurs in response to creation? Does Moltmann not risk losing the safeguards he has so carefully placed in *Trinity and the Kingdom*? Has he placed God and humanity within the same ontological horizon after all?

There may indeed be some slippage here. However, I think the more important point—as least as regards Moltmann's developing theology of place—is that the divine self-restriction functions as the point of contact between the trinitarian history and salvation history, between doxological theology and kerygmatic theology. Certainly, we can see how Moltmann would be concerned to provide such a point of contact, so allergic is he to any separation of God's identity from God's self-revelation in salvation history. And indeed, in Moltmann's explication of the Jewish doctrine of *zimsum*, he reflects on how God's "inward and outward aspects therefore correspond to one another and mirror one another."[39] *Zimsum*—an ancient Jewish doctrine, transformed by Isaac Luria[40] before being taken up by Moltmann—connotes "'concentration' or 'contraction', a withdrawal into the self."[41] Prior to there being any "outside" to God, God withdraws into godself. This withdrawal engenders and releases a nihil, a latency, a capacity for there to be something outside of—and other than—God. Moltmann quotes approvingly Luria's description of this latency as "'a kind of primal, mystical space'" into which can *subsequently* issue God's creation and revelation.[42] The self-limitation of God thus has dual aspect. Inasmuch as it takes place *ad intra*—for there is as of yet no *extra*—God alone undergoes it. Yet inasmuch as God's primal self-limitation throws open a space for creation, it is the inaugural work of salvation history.

Thus, if I understand Moltmann correctly, the correspondence between trinitarian history and salvation history is located here, where *ad intra*

---

39. Ibid., 110.
40. Ibid., 109.
41. Ibid.
42. Ibid., 110.

and *ad extra* coincide. I imagine Moltmann trying to chart a middle course; on the one hand, Moltmann is sharply critical of any model where salvation history and intra-trinitarian life run on parallel tracks. On the other hand, Moltmann is deliberately trying to avoid any hint of God's being exhaustively conditioned by an extra-divine horizon. Through his appropriation of *zimsum*, Moltmann maneuvers between these two infelicitous conclusions. God is limited—but not by an extra-divine horizon. Creation has a space thrown open for it—but it is a space within God. Trinitarian history and salvation history make contact, for God's self-restriction can be legitimately viewed under either aspect. But what of perichoresis? For all his talk of room making, Moltmann has so emphasized God's self-restriction that one is led to wonder: is there any room left for perichoresis? It would seem so, but it is not at all clear how this holds together with Moltmann's appeal to divine self-restriction. To be sure, Moltmann does discuss perichoresis, reflecting that that the divine Persons, "[B]y virtue of their eternal love . . . live in one another to such an extent, and dwell in one another to such an extent, that they are one."[43] If this is so, why the need for *zimsum*—a concept which arguably does a lot more real work in *Trinity and the Kingdom*?

Moltmann Considers Place

I shall now turn, at long last, to the explicit and sustained treatment Moltmann gives to place and space in his work from the late 1980's through the early 2000s. Specifically, I shall begin by looking at passages in *God in Creation* and *The Coming of God*, turning then to Moltmann's theological epistemology in *Experiences in Theology*. As I have mentioned, my appreciative critique of Moltmann proceeds on two fronts. First, I shall argue that the more richly placial elements of *God in Creation* are prevented from exercising their full power by Moltmann's other dialectical commitments. Second, I submit Moltmann is ambiguous about how perichoretic understandings of location (wherein quantities are able to co-inhere in the same location) square with restrictive understandings of location (wherein one quantity needs to make room for another). Do these map onto God and creation; and if so, how? Is God placed perichoretically, and creation restrictively? Are both God and creation placed restrictively, with perichoresis somehow becoming oddly non-placial? Or is there a sense in which both aspects of

---

43. Ibid., 175.

place show up in some fashion, whether we are talking about God's place or creation's place?

I begin with *God in Creation,* Moltmann's Gifford lectures from 1984–1985, and the major work of Moltmann's that most closely followed *Trinity and the Kingdom of God*. Moltmann's impetus, as he states in the opening, is the need for an "ecological doctrine of creation."[44] Moltmann intends to offer one which will correspond to the social doctrine of the trinity that he has developed in *The Trinity and the Kingdom*. In the pages that follow Moltmann emphasizes the similarity between created ecology and the trinity's sociality. By "ecology," Moltmann intends to evoke co-inherence, relationship, mutual influence, interconnectedness, symbiosis, and shared life.[45] In short order Moltmann signals that pneumatology will loom large in his ecological doctrine of creation. Citing Basil, Moltmann reminds us that "creation is a trinitarian process: the Father creates through the Son in the Holy Spirit . . . Everything that is, exists and lives in the unceasing inflow of the energies and potentialities of the cosmic Spirit."[46] Although Moltmann has not yet mapped pneumatology onto place explicitly, he does here indicate that something about creation's taking place *in the Spirit* grounds this buzzing, symbiotic, interconnected life that Moltmann calls "ecology." Presumably—since Moltmann has already said that his ecological doctrine of creation corresponds to the social doctrine of the trinity—the Spirit's role here corresponds to the role of the Spirit in the trinitarian history, as the one from whom the union of God proceeds.[47]

Moltmann's working-out of his ecological theology rests (as he has said it would) upon a correspondence between created ecology and social triunity, in a manner that fits well with the structure of *Trinity and the Kingdom*. Yet a simple correspondence between created ecology and social triunity will not take Moltmann as far as he wishes to go. Later Moltmann states that "[A]n ecological doctrine of creation," Moltmann stipulates, "implies a new kind of thinking about God. The centre of this thinking is no longer the distinction between God and the world. The centre is the recognition of the presence of God *in* the world and the presence of the world *in* God."[48] While hardly a dead giveaway, it seems to me—given the

44. Moltmann, *God in Creation*, 1.
45. Ibid., 3.
46. Ibid., 9.
47. Moltmann, *Trinity and the Kingdom*, 126.
48. Moltmann, *God in Creation*, 13.

The Place of the Spirit

context—that Moltmann does not want creation's ecology simply to *correspond* to God's sociality. Rather, he wants God and creation to share an ecology and a sociality. The implication is that the world and the triune God will coinhere within this buzzing, lively, animated horizon of ecological relationships.

Reading on, we find Moltmann making this point explicitly:

> God the Spirit is also the Spirit of the universe, its total cohesion, its structure, its information, its energy. The Spirit of the universe is the Spirit who proceeds from the Father and shines forth in the Son. The evolutions and the catastrophes of the universe are also the movements and experiences of the Spirit of creation.[49]

These conceptual moves evoke *Theology of Hope*, arguably, more than they do *Trinity and the Kingdom*. Moreover, the throwback to *Theology of Hope* occurs in a particular consideration of how the Spirit of God is present, placially, in the universe. Moltmann hints that the universe in some sense places the Spirit (for God is the Spirit of the universe), while the Spirit in some sense places the universe (by giving it cohesion and structure.) The relationship is dialectical, Moltmann tells us; and further, "[t]he archetype of this dialectical movement is to be found in the Godhead itself."[50] The dialectical movement involves God on the one hand, and "all relationships which are analogous to God" on the other. The dialectical structure situates "God *in* the world and the world *in* God; heaven and earth *in* the kingdom of God, pervaded by his glory; soul and body united *in* the life-giving Spirit to a human whole; woman and man *in* the kingdom of unconditional and unconditioned love."[51]

I have thus given one example of the first of the two aforementioned uncertainties that I see in Moltmann's discussions of place and space: whether to ground place in a theological framework of dialectic or correspondence. Yet the passages from *God in Creation* under discussion, for all their startling qualities, are at least consistent in their portrayal of perichoresis as an essential concept for a theology of place. To some extent, this is a departure from *Trinity and the Kingdom of God*. I noted earlier that, in *Trinity and the Kingdom*, Moltmann seemed to give less spatial and placial heft to perichoresis as a concept—at least as compared to *zimsum*. In

---

49. Ibid., 16.
50. Ibid.
51. Ibid., 17.

Trinity and the Kingdom, I argued, *zimsum* remains the main placial operator with respect to God; while perichoresis seems oddly thrown in.

Here, though—viewed through the lens of created ecology—perichoresis regains placial significance. For ecology evokes not only mutuality and relationship, but ecosystems and habitats. Thus when "ecology" is put forward here as the created counterpart to "perichoresis," the latter term tends to become placial by association, so to speak. The association persists later in *God in Creation*, in which Moltmann turns his attention to (as he titles the chapter) "The Space of Creation." Moltmann begins this reflection by noting the relative paucity of theological reflections on space compared to the voluminous theological reflection time.[52] He also traces the transition, in modernity, from a sense of space as "finite and self-contained, conceiv[ed] . . . in the image of 'the globe[,]'" to a sense of space as open, infinite, unlimited and eternal. Thus it would seem that the universe is, in modernity, given attributes of the divine—raising the question of whether "'the infinite universe' [is] a pantheistic name for the divine[.]" However, Moltmann points out, the modern person's sense of being located in an infinite eternal universe yields no triumph, no assurance. Rather, this sense "is the nihilistic sense of being lost, without anything to cling to, in the world's boundless emptiness: *horror vacui*."[53]

Thus, as has been the case so many times before, Moltmann's impetus is ethical; in discussing "the space of creation" Moltmann intends to address the sense of "metaphysical homelessness" plaguing modern women and men. To counter the *horror vacui*, Moltmann indicates, he will offer an "ecological concept of space," and in so doing address any number of questions about what, exactly, space is—whether it is an empty container, a category for perception, another name for the extension of objects, or an aspect of live ordered by our subjectivity (as in the expressions "living space" or "room to live in").[54] We would expect—given Moltmann's promise of an "ecological concept of space"—that he would indeed settle upon a definition of space relating to life, relationship, and subjectivity—and e would not be disappointed in this expectation. In the chapter entitled "The Space of Creation," Moltmann discussed the problems with the view of space as "empty, limitless vessel for objects," noting its origins in the

---

52. Ibid., 140.
53. Ibid., 141.
54. Ibid., 142.

difference conceptions of space in Plato and Aristotle[55] and the ossification into *res extensa* in Descartes.[56] He critiques this understanding, arguing instead for an understanding of space (which is the term Moltmann uses, not place) as overlaid with metaphors of life and indwelling. The cosmos, according to Moltmann's exegesis of the Priestly source, is created to contain "living spaces" for all the living creatures; and the Psalmist further testifies to the life-giving conditions that situate humans and beasts, meeting their creaturely needs.[57] Too, there is a sense in which God can dwell in creation—through mutual indwelling and participation. In fact, I think it is fair to say that, in *God in Creation*, Moltmann now displays a growing tendency to use perichoresis as the placial term of choice, when discussing how God and creation relate to each other in spatial and placial horizons. To make the most of this connection between place and perichoresis, Moltmann is willing to let slide some of the stipulations he had built into *Trinity and the Kingdom*. But then let us compare the preceding treatment of space and place, to the one Moltmann composes ten years later in *The Coming of God*, and we see a seeming hesitation. Here, in introducing the "theological problems of space," for example, Moltmann does not begin with as think a description of what space is. Rather, he returns to the question of how there can be an *ad extra* to God. Moltmann did not invent this theological question, of course, and to an extent this reproduces the discussion that took place in *Trinity and the Kingdom*. Note, though, how it has become hardened compared to his earlier work. In *Trinity and the Kingdom*, the possibility of an "outside" to God was threatened by God's identity as Love, as the triune self-communication of the good. Such a God might, it was suggested, exhaust all possibilities for relationship. Here, though, the problem is introduced in terms of God's *omnipresence*; "if God is omnipresent, can there be an 'outside' for him—an outside which must, after all, be assumed if we talk about the *opera Dei ad extra*?"[58] The question is not only whether there is room for creation, but whether God can act freely upon an arena other than himself. In other words, the problem lies not just in there being "room" for creation, but for God. Moltmann goes on to cite Dmitru Staniloae's contention that "[e]very space is restricted, and restricts. Every

---

55. Ibid., 145–46.
56. Ibid., 147–48.
57. Ibid., 148.
58. Moltmann, *Coming of God*, 296–97.

space creates distance."[59] Therefore the only "room" that God can carve out—the only way in which God can make a primordial horizon in which to act—is by restricting godself.

Place and Theological Method in Experiences in Theology

In *Experiences in Theology*, the final volume of his "Contributions" series, Moltmann sets out to give his theological method, and in the course of so doing discusses his theological epistemology. He acknowledges in the preface that this reverses the typical order. Usually a systematic theology begins with prolegomena, in which "the method chosen and the understanding of theology presupposed are all discussed."[60] Moltmann explains that he avoided that approach, partly out of a general suspicion of the modern project of shoring up a now-dubious discipline of theology by investing in prolegomena "try[ing] to answer the fundamental questions with the help of whatever new philosophy, psychology, or science of religion is at hand."[61] Too, Moltmann divulges that "[u]p to now these questions about method have not greatly interested [him]," because he "wanted to get to know the real content of theology."[62] His turn to method, he explains, coincided with his growing appreciation for the "conditions and limitations of his own place, and the relativity of his own context. It is impossible to say anything that is theologically valid for everyone at all times and in all places."[63] Engaging with readers of his work—both appreciative and critical—enabled him, he explains, to appreciate the intersection of his context and his approach to theology. Thus, to hear Moltmann tell it, his turn to method coincided with his turn to place chronologically, but perhaps also conceptually. In *Experiences in Theology* he treats both broad topics and the connections between them, in the process interrogating as well his own theological location[64]

---

59. Ibid., 297.
60. Moltmann, *Experiences in Theology*, xiv.
61. Ibid.
62. Ibid.
63. Ibid., xvii.
64. This is the focus of section III in Moltmann, *Experiences in Theology*, "Mirror Images of Liberating Theology," in which he considers liberation theologies from his own standpoint as a white, first world, economically privileged man.

The Place of the Spirit

In chapter four, on theological epistemology, Moltmann considers several different models for knowing God. Although he considers the strengths of each, he discloses at the outset that this chapter is an exercise in advocacy. "We shall begin," he says, "with the Aristotelian axiom that 'like can only be known by like', and examine the ways in which human beings, who are not like God, try to know God[.]"[65] So far, this latter admission of human beings' discontinuity with God squares with that of the patristic theologians we examined in the previous chapter—although its subsequent spelling-out may not (a possibility I shall consider momentarily). But then Moltmann allows that "[w]e shall then develop the counter-axiom, that in reality 'only the unlike can know each other', and shall consider the dialectical knowing of God[.]"[66] However irenic Moltmann's consideration of each mode of theological knowing—likeness, analogy, metaphor, apophasis, dialectic, counter-images, and sacrament—Moltmann has announced at the outset that this chapter will argue for the dialectical model.

In the subsequent discussion, only certain of the models have placial implications, and so I shall focus presently on those: the principles of likeness, analogy, dialectic, and counter-images (or more specifically counter-worlds, which Moltmann treats as a particularly compelling instance of counter-images).[67] The principle of likeness, of which Moltmann is the most critical, is a principle with a pedigree going back to Aristotle. "Ever since Aristotle," Moltmann recalls, "the cognitive principle has been 'Like is only known by like.'" Moltmann criticizes this model for excluding, on principle, anything in the other which does not "accord . . . with ourselves[.]" Through such knowing "[w]e adopt for ourselves what fits in with ourselves, but do not change to understand what is different."[68] Strikingly, Moltmann expresses this in the language of "external world" and "in-

65. Moltmann, *Experiences in Theology*, 151.

66. Ibid.

67. Those which remain are metaphor, apophasis, and sacrament. Briefly, Moltmann envisions metaphorical knowledge to destabilize conceptual knowledge, acting as mini-parables, and "throw[ing] open the realm of possibilities" foreclosed on by strict concepts. (*Experiences in Theology*, 162) Of negative theology, Moltmann notes that its purpose is to resist anthropomorphic talk about God (166); but cautions against saying that unknowability itself is a divine attribute. "We can no doubt say that God is unknowable," he clarifies, "but not that unknowability is divine. The negations . . . can just as well be applied to what is deadly" (169). Sacramental knowing pertains to "faith-creating word[s]" (177), where God speaks in the human Word, with the power and authority for the words found in the indwelling power of the Spirit (178).

68. Moltmann, *Experiences in Theology*, 152.

ner world." "All knowledge of phenomena in the external world perceived through the senses evokes a resonance in the inner world, if the phenomena are received[,]" he explains. "If they evoke resistance and contradiction, they will not be perceived at all, not even perceived."[69] The fact that Moltmann here speaks of two realms—an external world and an inner world, with knowledge being posited as a coherence between the two—might not be so suggestive, were it not for the fact that he thereby also frames the model which he *does* advocate: the dialectical model of knowing. As we shall shortly see, the dialectical model likewise assumes two domains which transcend themselves by opening to, and including within themselves, the other. Put to theological use, of course, this looks a great deal like Moltmann's understanding of perichoresis—within the trinity, but also between God and creation.

That discussion is postponed, however, in favor of Moltmann's consideration of *analogia entis*.[70] According to this model, human creatures "cannot . . . deduce the Creator and his attributes from creation and its attributes," but rather "creation as a whole can be understood as a parable of the creator."[71] The idea, I gather, is that creation refers in a non-totalizing way to God's self-disclosure in creation, without thereby collapsing God into creation. In this way "everything created is open towards God" but "God is the One who, above and beyond his parable-like reflection, is 'always greater.'"[72] Moltmann criticizes this model as being too concerned with the possibility of knowledge, rather than with present suffering. "The doctrine . . . says nothing[,]" he asserts, "about the knowledge of God of the truly Godless and Godforsaken[.]"[73] This is a problem, for Moltmann, because God is in fact "here and now," with us, acting for our sakes and for the sakes (perhaps even especially) of those who experience God's absence. By focusing so much on the abstract possibility of knowledge about God, and the conditions under which such knowledge might be possible, *analogia entis* makes claims about fixed notions of Creator and creature. Moltmann contends that a truly satisfactory understanding of theological knowledge would not focus on humanity in the abstract—let alone the conditions under which a theoretical human could know God—but rather on the Spirit's

69. Ibid.
70. Ibid., 156.
71. Ibid.
72. Ibid., 157.
73. Ibid.

The Place of the Spirit

activity alleviating "the sufferings and sighings of an enslaved creation," creating anew even in the midst of abjection.[74]

Here again, Moltmann foreshadows what will ultimately be his preference—the dialectic model of knowledge. But at this point Moltmann seems to change his approach somewhat. Although the subject is ostensibly knowledge of God, Moltmann now begins discussing "closeness" rather than knowledge. This follows on the heels of his assertion that *analogia entis* ignores, to too great a degree, the way in which God is actually acting towards the godforsaken—preferring instead to surmise the conditions of possibility for knowledge about God, in the abstract. But in his rejoinder, and particularly in his appeal to closeness, is Moltmann still any longer discussing knowledge? God is acting toward the despondent and the abject, and therefore—he seems to suggest—God is close to them. But closeness turns out not to track with knowledge. Indeed, the opposite is the case: "[T]he closer we come to God," he says, "or—better—the closer God comes to us, the more unknowable for us he is. Strangeness is a category not of distance but of *closeness*[.]"[75] Closeness is strange, Moltmann suggests, because it disturbs the safe remove that representational knowledge affords. Representations—whether picture or image—"create . . . a distance of this kind."[76] By contrast, the "all-interpenetrating" activity of the Spirit creates a closeness which resists representation. Therefore (the implication seems to be) God is available even to those for whom God seems, intellectually, to be absent. Under the condition of such closeness, "God is then so present to us that we are in God."[77] Again, Moltmann foreshadows his eventual preference for dialectical knowing, using the spatial language of distance and closeness. The experience of God's absence, Moltmann suggests, actually coincides with God's closeness—a closeness so profound that it cannot be detected because it is God whom the godforsaken one is already in. Interestingly, Moltmann invokes Augustine here as one who saw, in God's apparent unknowability, God's closeness—based on Augustine's understanding that God is "closer to us than we ourselves can come."[78] But in the passage of the *Confessions* which Moltmann cites—III, 6, 11—Augustine also mentions that he was wandering far from God, even as God was close. In my

---

74. Ibid., 158–59.
75. Ibid., 160.
76. Ibid.
77. Ibid.
78. Ibid.

opinion, this strikes a different placial note—and indeed, an altogether different theological note—from Moltmann's more straightforward schema of interpenetration, wherein God is so present to us that we are in God.

But of course, Moltmann is precisely making a case for dialectical knowing, wherein two quantities realize themselves by overstepping themselves and including an other, and this informs his criticism of *analogia entis* as well as his appropriation of Augustine. At last he treats dialectical knowing head-on, and the placial images are resonant. "[I]t is only in the foreign land[,]" he asserts, "that we discover what home is." The placial images of "foreign land" and "homeland" recall Moltmann's prior discussion of distance. In the preceding discussion of analogical knowledge, the "distance" had signaled representational knowledge about God, and "closeness" God's unknowability. Here, however, "distance" signals the alterity essential to self-realization. For "[i]t is first in the *distance*, even more in the *difference*, and then finally in the contradiction that we perceive the other, and in perceiving that other at the same time perceive our own selves."[79] Corresponding to the two quantities of "self" and "other" are two domains, whose dialectical relationship Moltmann describes using the language of boundary crossing. As was not the case for Gregory of Nyssa, this boundary seems to apply to both God and creatures—perhaps not equally or even univocally, but in a way that requires God to cross it as part of being God. Corresponding to and grounding the process that enables us to be in God, Moltmann explains, revelation "is the divine crossing of the frontier into the human existence which is 'other' for God and into the human misery of sin which contradicts him."[80] Considering that Moltmann began this section by announcing that he would argue for an epistemological model in which "only the unlike can know each other," the overall effect of this chapter is to strongly suggest that God realizes godself by crossing the boundary separating God's domain, and traversing into the domain of creation.

Moltmann thus gives a different picture than the Cappadocians or Augustine. Can it truly be said, though, that Moltmann is here arguing for an understanding wherein place overwhelmingly designates a preconstituted expanse? I offer two responses to this objection. First, if I understand Moltmann correctly, he understands himself to have accounted for this—by grounding interpenetration/perichoresis in the relationships between the three Persons. This strategy, I take it, is meant to lend trinitarian priority;

79. Ibid., 171.
80. Ibid., 172.

The Place of the Spirit

the dialectical relationships between Father, Son, and Spirit ground the fact that God realizes godself by crossing creation's boundary. Ultimately, though, I think that even this claim of trinitarian priority relies upon an unsatisfactory placial model—as I shall explain shortly. However, there is one element in Moltmann's epistemology which *is* placial in the manner I find most theologically useful, although this placiality is underdetermined. Moltmann's notion of "counter-worlds," a subset of "counter-images," evokes the world-constructing aspect of place which I have been arguing for. Moltmann, not surprisingly, dwells on the oppositional nature of counter-images—their capacity to resist totalitarian and tyrannical spaces and places by creating subversive counter-worlds where resistance is possible.[81] What strikes me, in light of my own aims, is how Moltmann here allows that placing the world involves structuring it and endowing it with meaning—whether we are creating a space of resistance or simply "detach[ing] ourselves from the reality at hand in order to imagine . . . counter-worlds[.]" The activity of structuring an already found world by means of symbols and images, the result of which informs how one may live in the world; this placial understanding squares more nearly with the "placial advocacy" models we came across in chapter one. However, one cannot make much more of this element of Moltmann's work, as it is treated so briefly, and not especially thematically.

When—in the later section entitled "The 'Broad Place' of the Trinity—Moltmann does thematize place, the domain model dominates. Helpfully, Moltmann explains the rationale behind his recent turn to place. His earlier work, he now realizes, "had been one-sided in its orientation towards time. I now tried to extend it through the concepts of space and 'home', the Shekinah and the perichoresis[.]"[82] Following Latin tradition, he says, he distinguishes two moments in perichoresis: *circumincession* (meaning "a dynamic interpenetration") and *circuminsessio* (meaning an "enduring, resting indwelling.")[83] These two moments of dynamism and rest may be described—quite straightforwardly, it seems—with the language of passivity and activity. "Each Person[,]" Moltmann argues, "actively dwells in the two others and passively cedes space for the two others—that is to say, at

81. Ibid., 175.
82. Ibid., 314.
83. Ibid., 316. Notably the Cappadocian *periphera* seems to have dropped out of the discussion, although whether this is due to Moltmann's own theological preferences or to the Latin tradition he draws from, I am unsure.

once gives and receives the others[.]"[84] Moltmann does not make a point of saying that passivity and activity are processes recognized by a finite intellect, and apply only in a qualified sense to God. To the contrary, the intra-trinitarian dynamic of passivity and activity seem to occasion the Persons' self-realization. Being given room by the two other Persons allows each Person to "come . . . to himself and become conscious of himself." The Father comes to himself and becomes conscious of himself in the Son and the Spirit; the Son likewise in the Father and the Spirit; and the Spirit in the Father and the Son.[85] The language of "ceding space" naturally signals a spatialized understanding. This is all the more emphasized by the language of passivity and activity. What is particularly striking here is that it fits so well with Moltmann's earlier preference for a dialectical model of theological knowledge. Again, my sense is that Moltmann means for this intra-trinitarian dialectic to provide grounding for the (on his view) subsequent dialectical model for knowing God. Such trinitarian priority would presumably act as a hedge against the charge that Moltmann entirely subsumes the trinity to intra-mundane categories. In my opinion, however, Moltmann's spatializing tendencies undercut such a goal. Indeed, space—at least, a kind of space—threatens to overtake both God and the cosmos as the final situater. It seems as though, for Moltmann, God realizes godself by traversing a domain that includes both God and creation. Prior to that, the Persons realize themselves by traversing a domain in which passivity and activity operate, an arena which provides the arena for perichoresis. I do not see where the arenas themselves, or passivity and activity, are in turn grounded in triunity. To the contrary, Moltmann's stated preference for trinitarian dialectic evidently requires that these operations condition the trinitarian relations themselves.

Moltmann's Contributions to a Trinitarian Theology of Place

In the final analysis, it seems to me as though Moltmann offers several positive features of use in building a trinitarian theology of place. The most obvious, of course, is that Moltmann considers place explicitly, and explicitly connects it to triunity. In *God in Creation* Moltmann's discussion of space evokes some of the best elements of the placial retrieval—particularly its

84. Moltmann, *Experiences in Theology*, 318.
85. Ibid., 319.

The Place of the Spirit

critique of infinite, totalized, punctuate, passive, space. Moltmann offers space in which life is lived, beings dwell together, and coinherence is possible . . . and he does so in a trinitarian idiom. Moreover, Moltmann's work shows the fruitful possibilities for connecting triunity to created spaces and places. I think he is quite right, for example, in linking Trinitarian thought to ecology. His use of placial images and traditions drawn from Judaism are particularly instructive. And even the more problematic aspects of Moltmann's theology demonstrate a central point of this dissertation, namely the degree to which the question "How are place and trinity related?" bumps up against the question "How do we know God?"

At the same time, there are elements of Moltmann's thought, having to do specifically with place, which do not hold together altogether satisfactorily. Moltmann wishes to retain divine self-restriction as a hedge against the possibility that God and creation wind up placed within the same horizon. Yet Moltmann seems to find it difficult, within that framework, to say all that he wants to say about the mutual indwelling of God and creation, or how this mutual indwelling is grounded in the prior indwelling of the three persons. Faced with this problem, Moltmann reverts again to perichoresis, but does so inconsistently and without explaining why he has done so. Moreover, in his theological epistemology, both perichoresis and creaturely knowledge about God prove to be dialectical in ways that pose problems. Both perichoresis and theological knowledge require God and creation—and, before that, Father, Son, and Spirit—to go outside of themselves in order to realize themselves. In this sense Moltmann is consistent; the elements of his thought follow a similar logic and movement. And perhaps Moltmann is not overly bothered by the fact that dialectic, passivity, activity, and spatiality tend to condition God in an ultimate sense. As one interested in constructing a trinitarian theology of place, however, I do find this concerning. To allow such variables to condition God straightforwardly raises the obvious theological question: why not grant these terms, and not God, theological ultimacy? In addition, this model leaves Moltmann in a poor position to address the critiques—such as those I discussed in chapter one—of the type of spatiality which seems to undergird his theological model. What if location does not have to do with passive, fully realized, preconstituted expanses? What if—following Heidegger, Bachelard, and Tuan—it has more to do with world-structuring? What will become of perichoresis?

None of this is meant to disparage or downplay the significance of Moltmann's having treated place explicitly. Moltmann offers a thorough and creative description of how trinity looks if a certain understanding of place—a domain, albeit one full of life and interconnectivity—is deployed. My next interlocutor, Jean-Luc Marion, offers what in one sense is the precise opposite. Marion gives us a trinity in which any domain for God, and by association, any place, is absolutely, utterly, endlessly refused. He gives what I consider to be an extreme and reified version of the all-situating, yet un-situated, trinity. Needless to say, his interests and aims are quite different from Moltmann's. As we turn to Marion's work, let us bear in mind the strengths and problems of Moltmann's model, and finally explore how the two might correct each other.

4

No Place for the Spirit? Jean-Luc Marion's Placial Refusal

Placial Refusal

"PATERNAL DISTANCE," WRITES JEAN-LUC MARION, "OFFERS THE SOLE place for a filiation."[1] But what sort of distance is this, and what kind of placing is appropriate to it? Does it in fact have, span, or mark off any place, however understood? Or is distance, rather, exactly a *refusal* of any location, circumscription or horizon? Or does Marion in fact answer both of these questions in the affirmative—thus ascribing a tense, changeable, and not entirely consistent placing to this over freighted "distance"?

These questions point to various possibilities for how to read Marion on place. The issue of place itself, however, is raised by Marion, albeit usually implicitly. For one thing, Marion invests his targets—the totalizing tendencies of metaphysics, and the idolatrous gaze generally—with placial language, to the degree that one could conclude that being placed and being conditioned are, if not the same thing, at least closely related. Moreover, distance—arguably Marion's most central theological category—is a placial term, and not, I suggest, incidentally. Marion's project is expounded in placial terms because, in fact, Marion has a lot to say about placing, about horizons, and about the vulnerability of placed human creatures to build idols that suit the places in which they live. Thus on the one hand, Marion seems to see a strong link between locating horizons, metaphysics, and idolatry—rendering place a very inappropriate category for God. On the

---

1. Marion, *Idol and Distance*, 139.

other hand, Marion correctly perceives the need to not simply deny that God is placed, but to return a christological placing that is not idolatrous. Offering theological "sites" in exchange for idolatrous "horizons" seems, to me, to be Marion's attempt to rehabilitate place. In my opinion, however, this attempt is not successful; Marion's "sites" may seem to be place recuperated, but stubbornly lapse into being straightforward refusals of place. That is, they point to God's being outside of *prior* horizons, as well they should—but they also sneak in a straightforward denial that paternal-filial distance is in any sense located. The refusal of location, in other words, paradoxically becomes the locating feature for christology. This raises problems on two fronts. First, Marion suggests that straightforward, categorical negations about God do not escape idolatry. What, then, are we to make of the implicit negation, "God is not placed," which seems to crop up in his work? Second, and more centrally, Marion's implicit assertion paternal-filial distance is not located, in any sense, seems to raise serious questions about whether Marion's theological universe gives the Holy Spirit any room whatsoever.

I shall spend sections two examining the strange status that place assumes in *Idol and Distance*. I shall suggest that, in this work, Marion has not yet straightforwardly denied placing of God, although he certainly leaves the door open to this interpretation by tending to associate being placed with being conditioned. Then I shall turn to *Prolegomena to Charity* and *God Without Being*, and argue that Marion hardens his stance regarding place—even as he tries to recuperate it by offering trinitarian and Eucharistic sites. Finally I shall evaluate whether this recuperation is theologically satisfactory. In my negative answer I shall point out the two problems I mention above. First, Marion risks denying something of God—that God is in any sense placed—in a way that according to his own criteria risks becoming idolatrous. Therefore, unlike many other categories which, in Marion's work, are radically refigured in light of christology—Being, the concept, the divine Name, and so forth—place remains oddly unreconstructed and unredeemed. Second, Marion allows paternal-filial distance to operate in such a way that the Holy Spirit cannot show up except as a power of the Son or a modifier of distance. In his freighting of paternal-filial distance between the Father and the Son, filiation ends up being so inexhaustible abyss that there remains no possibility for spiration. And in fact, Marion has very little to say about the third person of the trinity; there is a real sense in which a binary God would be better suited to Marion's task. If this is the case, then Marion's trinitarian theology, at the very least, would need to be remediated in order to bear witness to the triune God whom, one assumes, he intends to confess.

I do believe such a remediation is not only possible but highly desirable, for there is much to recommend Marion's project. For one thing, Marion's negative evaluation of idolatrous placing, and his attendant attempt to offer redeemed (if non-placial) sites for theology, invites one to consider whether non-objectifying, transformed, redeemed placiality might be possible. (This has additional benefit for someone who—unlike Marion, one presumes—is troubled by some of the gendered associations that have persistently attended place in the west. Marion offers theological tools to think place apart from passivity, for example.) In addition, admitting a placial term into trinitarian discourse goes a long way toward developing a fleshed-out Christian theology of place. For Marion, crucially, paternal-filial distance is not something other than the Father's self-gift in love—that is to say, the Son. Marion thus manages to avoid either an extra-divine backdrop or, alternately, an intra-trinitarian clearing or interval. The precise way in which Marion tried to avoid such an interval, in my opinion, causes problems for pneumatology. Nevertheless, anyone trying to ground created place in trinitarian discourse will do well to build upon Marion's central insights. Moreover, the fact that the problems with Marion's scheme correlate with problems in pneumatology further raises a tantalizing possibility: that if one is to get a roomy trinity, one will need especially to link place with pneumatology.

Placing Marion

Before discussing possibilities for location and placing in Marion's theology, I ought first to attempt to locate Marion by mentioning the conversations in which he takes part, and to which his theological project refers. Briefly put, Marion mounts a defense of theology against a host of recent philosophical problems surrounding being, presence, and gift. Working in the continental tradition, Marion takes over from Heidegger and Levinas a sensitivity to the ways in which universal being has been applied and the interests this application has served. He, like they, is suspicious of the metaphysical agenda that corrals all particular beings into the confinement of some shared universal Being and locates their intelligibility there. Marion shares the related fear that metaphysics thus serves to deny particularity and alterity, precludes ethics, and is motivated by the violent desire to subsume all Others to the Same.[2] In *The Idol and Distance* and *God Without Being*, Marion concerns himself in particular with the ways in which God has befallen (and not befallen) this fate. Those who have proclaimed God's death, Marion suggests, are in a sense correct; but it is only the conceptual idol of ontotheology, the Highest Being, who has died. (How he makes this case, I shall discuss in a moment.)

Marion also takes seriously the anxieties behind Derrida's project of deconstruction. In particular, Marion sees himself as responding to Derrida's insight that it is no longer possible to imagine the currency of language being anywhere backed up by presence. To the contrary, the economy of signs is built upon a foundation of absence, of re-presenting as present what is not present. Moreover, according to Derrida, once one attends to the temporality of language one must conclude that a sign's meaning is determined in light of the total number of times it has been used; and so with each iteration the meaning changes.[3] The economic aspect of language also bears upon the phenomenality of the gift—another point to which Marion responds. Both Derrida and Levinas, in slightly different ways, have pointed out that the conditions of possibility for the appearance of gift seem also to be the conditions of its impossibility.[4] To name the criteria that a true gift must meet (freely given, no thought of reward, anonymous) is to put gift within the economy of signs; but within the economy of signs those very criteria cannot be met. It is therefore impossible for a gift to appear as such. Marion responds to all of these insights, but before noting his response it is worth marking the difference between his theological and phenomenological works on exactly this point. In his phenomenological work Marion is concerned to show the possibility of the phenomenon of gift, where in his theological works he aims to show that there has, in fact, been a revelation in which a gift has been given.[5]

---

2. See, for example, a characteristic passage in "The Intentionality of Love" in which Marion poses the question, "What can I ever love outside of myself, given that the progress of loving consists in reducing all alterity to myself, under the figure of the represented?" Marion, *Prolegomena to Charity*, 71–72.

3. This is discussed in, among other places, Derrida's essay "Différance," in Derrida, *Margins of Philosophy*, 1–27.

4. For a summary of the issues and persons involved in the debate see also Horner, *Rethinking God as Gift: Marion, Derrida, and the Limits of Phenomenology* and Caputo and Scanlon, *God, the Gift, and Postmodernism*.

5. Carlson, introduction to Marion, *Idol and Distance*, xii–xiii.

The Place of the Spirit

As a Christian theologian, Marion must make a case for the gift having been truly given without becoming subject to the economic laws of exchange that govern signs. In addition (and obviously, the two go hand in hand) he must make a case for an absolute presence that truly discloses itself, without denying that language will be unable to signify this presence. In fact Marion does make these moves, and does so christologically. As the Son is related to the Father without being other than the Father, and as Jesus Christ truly takes on humanity without compromising divinity, so in turn is the gift truly given without thereby becoming subject to economy, and so is God's presence truly disclosed without our thereby being able to predicate something of it as of an object.[6] This coincidence of God's presence and God's absence occurs before being,[7] in the Father's primordial giving of the Son.[8] The "paternal distance" between the Father and the Son—the otherness in God that admits relation—generates a dynamic love that abounds in its very withdrawal.[9] This paternal distance, in turn, grounds the distance between God and creation that allows for the gift of created being, which is neither the same as God nor other than God.

Indeed, this distance *is* itself the gift of creaturely being (inasmuch as it admits relation to God of what is not God), and as such is both a disclosure and a withdrawal. Disclosure, because God truly discloses God's love in the giving of being; and withdrawal, because this love refuses all predication and conceptual nailing-down. The result is an apophatic dispossession, even death, of predicative discourse that can never comprehend or exhaust the divine love that makes it possible.[10] Beyond this death, however, is yet another christological correlation: resurrection. In Christ, the Word of God made flesh, the unthinkable has been incarnated in the thinkable;[11] and as Christ is resurrected from the dead, so may our shifting, self-enclosed predicative discourse be (after the apophatic death) "resurrected" into ceaseless (and, so Marion claims, non-predicative) praise.[12] Because what has been

---

6. Marion, *Idol and Distance*, 139: "It is not a question of speaking the supreme Being within a predication of which it would be the object."

7. Marion, *God without Being*, 75–76.

8. Marion, *Idol and Distance*, 146.

9. Ibid., 139.

10. Ibid., 139–145.

11. And in this sense was foreshadowed by the giving to Israel of the tetragrammaton, the unspeakable name of God (see ibid., 140ff.) I shall treat this in greater depth later.

12. Ibid., 144–45. My highlighting of only this aspect of Marion's christology runs the risk of suggesting that he pays no attention to sin. His understanding of sin is beyond the

given is precisely the unthinkable (God's inexhaustible love that yields both distance and relation), the gift is not subject to the economy of exchange that would render it impossible. And because the gift that yields creaturely being stands before and beyond it, the Giver as well remains beyond being

Place and Distance in Idol and Distance

The above brief sketch says nothing about Marion's explicit treatment of place, and that is largely because place is not explicitly treated. Yet it does show up, and in ways that touch upon the issues mentioned above—presence, the gift, and distance most centrally. In *Idol and Distance*, the first of the three works under consideration, Marion exhibits a striking ambivalence about placing and God—but this ambivalence does not become hardened into a straightforward denial as it does, I suggest, in the two later works. Let me begin by rehearsing some of the central concerns of *Idol and Distance*, as they are laid out in the first essay—which Marion has given the tantalizingly placial title of "The Marches of Metaphysics," and which, in fact, is arguably his most explicit treatment of place. Marion's begins with an opening question intended as a rejoinder to death-of-God theologians; rather than declaring that God is dead, Marion says, he will ask "with greater reason and profit, under what conditions the statement 'God is dead,' becomes, or remains, thinkable."[13] In due time, and with more finesse than I am able to do justice to here, Marion answers the death of God is possible when the "God" in question is a particular sort of quantity—namely, the sort of "God" whom one thinks in terms of death, for whom death is the fixed reality in relation to which God is defined. If the death-of-God theologians err by thinking God in terms of death (or anything else), Marion points out, it is only because there was already good precedent for them to do so. After all, onto-theology commits an equivalent error when—as the theological realization of metaphysics—it posits God in terms of the given quantity of Being, rather than allowing God to stand at "the center

---

scope of this paper, but the relevant work would be "Evil in Person," the first chapter of *Prolegomena to Charity*, in which Marion discusses the logic of iniquity, its relentless and unfailing transmission, and the manner in which Christ allows the full force of the logic of iniquity to befall him without in turn passing it on. The risk Christ takes (in bearing all evil but refusing to pass it on) results in his death. (See especially *Prolegomena to Charity*, 9–10).

13. Marion, *Idol and Distance*, 1.

The Place of the Spirit

of a discourse that orders itself in relation to him."[14] The problem is, as Heidegger has already pointed out, this criticism applies to much of Christian discourse. For "[i]t would," Marion says, "be a little too visibly facile to oppose a 'true' God to the 'God' of onto-theology since, in fact, for us, the one and the other are historically imbricated."[15] Therefore Marion must ask if it is even possible for Christian discourse to be salvaged—for Christian theology to "advance outside of ontotheology[,]"[16] to "take onto-theology into view starting from what, in Christianity, might escape it?"[17]

These are, in broad strokes, the moves Marion makes in the opening sections of "The Marches of Metaphysics." The placial imagery abounds, as early as the title. By "marches," Marion explains, he has in mind "limits" which "do not only delimit a territory" but "defend it, like a glacis, a line of fortifications . . . They also surround it, an already foreign territory, exposed to danger, half-unknown."[18] This image—that of a territory whose delimitation consists in its being defended from the dangers that surround it—goes a long way towards framing the central argument I have attempted to sketch, above. "Territory" evokes many of Marion's criticisms of metaphysic the hubris, the totalizing tendency, the dominating episteme. But by investigating this territory's fragile borders—indeed, by stipulating that it has borders in the first place—Marion exposes its vulnerability. If Marion is correct, then metaphysic's defenses turn out to open onto something wider, giving the lie to its totalizing claims and affording access to those half-unknown "border territories" which Marion will explore in the rest of *Idol and Distance*.

How much weight ought one put on the fact that Marion's choice of imagery here is a placial one? Is the placiality of territory, and its status as figure for metaphysics, only incidental to his project? In light of what Marion says about idols, it would seem not. To understand why, one must note the particular way in which idolatry and metaphysics are bound up in each other. The specific idolatrous error of metaphysics—thinking God in terms of something else—is, for Marion, a special instance of the more general idolatrous error of placing God within a horizon. In the case of an idol—whether made of stone or of concepts—Marion writes, "the divine

14. Ibid., 4.
15. Ibid., 17.
16. Ibid., 18.
17. Ibid., 20–21.
18. Ibid., 19.

always already belongs to my sphere, as an idol that is close and, for that very reason, vain."[19] What I am suggesting here, is that Marion performs two moves which, taken together, cast location and placing in a negative theological light. First, Marion links God's being conditioned with God's being located within a horizon. In other words, Marion's beef is with the conceptual idolatry of metaphysics; but, crucially, he exposes metaphysics as idolatrous precisely by showing it to be a refined version of idol making, of forcing the divine to show up within one's own sphere. Second, Marion seems to hold any such prior horizon will inevitably be a front for human projection. God's being conditioned, coupled with God's being *placed* within a prior horizon, is in turn coupled with God's being *projected* from human experience. This is the God whom Nietzsche (rightly, on Marion's view) calls dead.

One might well ask how, if the claims of metaphysics are so overreaching and totalizing, one could ever perceive metaphysics to be a delimited territory at all. Presumably Marion writes to those of us whom he believes to stand within this heavily fortified territory, formed as we (and he) are by western philosophy. From what vantage point is he—from what vantage point are we—able to see this territory from without? Marion raises this issue himself when he says that must "to take onto-theology up again from the place where we are. We undoubtedly cannot get out of it."[20] To have any hope of viewing metaphysics and onto-theology rightly—to perceive its limits and hubris—we must "travel through onto-theology itself all along its limits . . . [t]o take onto-theology tangentially, from the angle of its lines of defense, and thus to expose oneself to what already no longer belongs to it."[21] As it turns out, we do not, strictly speaking, view the territory from without; we only proceed tangentially, along its edges. But it is here that placial language begins to strain. For we do—or at least, Marion does—need to affirm that there is a reality outside the territory the aforementioned "border territories" of Nietzsche's, Hölderlin's, and Denys' thought, certainly, but much more fundamentally and in a radically different way, God. If God cannot be found within this horizon—if that would be tantamount to idolatry—then God must be in some sense without. But God cannot be "outside" metaphysics in any naïve sense. It's not the case, so to speak, that we just need a bigger map covering an even more expansive

19. Ibid., 7.
20. Ibid., 19.
21. Ibid.

The Place of the Spirit

area. Marion's whole point, after all, has been that we do not plot "God" according to a prior set of coordinates. Therefore, the sense in which God is outside—the placiality of this "outside"—will have to be parsed carefully.

Enter distance. Whereas "an idol . . . is close and, for that very reason, vain,"[22] distance provides some measure of non-idolatrous location. Distance, moreover, is on Marion's view central to the thought of the three thinkers he engages is *Idol and Distance*. It appears as "a distance outside of onto-theology for Nietzsche, a filially received distance of the presence of a God who is paternally in withdrawal for Hölderlin, and a distance traversed liturgically toward the Requisite by the discourse of praise of requestants for Denys."[23] I cannot here summarize, let alone do justice to, Marion's readings of Nietzsche, Hölderlin, and Denys, but I will offer a few observations about the placiality of distance as it specifically appears in these three essays in *Idol and Distance*. (Obviously, there will be much more to say about distance in the other two works as well.)

In the Nietzsche essay, Marion mentions that Nietzsche's thought creates a "space—an empty space" that is "free[d] up" by the death of the idols.[24] This space is desolate in the extreme. Marion describes it as "a desertion . . . an evacuation . . . gaping, fascinating in that degree, and all the more demanding."[25] This placial image seems to me to sum up all that Marion finds worthwhile—and all that Marion finds still tainted with idolatry—in Nietzsche's work. As Marion points out in "Interlude 1" an empty space that "delivers, more than a desert, the anonymous space of an anarchic invasion of the divine,"[26] is still after all a horizon against which God shows up. Which is to say that even an utter, gaping emptiness—one so defined by its passivity that it practically requires a corresponding all powerful force to "invade" it "anarchically"—gives too much placial determination to the divine for Marion's taste. This corresponds precisely to Marion's encounter with Nietzsche. According to Marion, Nietzsche himself did not ultimately rid himself of metaphysics. Rather, "Nietzschean distance maintains . . . a relation with the divine, but within onto-theology," by "reinforc[ing] the metaphysical idolatry where 'God' is defined as a state of the will to power."[27]

22. Ibid., 7.
23. Ibid., 21.
24. Ibid., 36.
25. Ibid.
26. Ibid., 79
27. Ibid., 77.

No Place for the Spirit? Jean-Luc Marion's Placial Refusal

At the same time—with Nietzsche, as with the desolation he inaugurates—we do see here an authentic deviation from onto-theology and metaphysics, according to Marion. Room is, after all, freed up when the idols are cleared out; the empty, passive space left behind is much less placially determined than, say, a territory. It would be preliminary to state this yet as a general principle, but nevertheless this example does reinforce a certain pattern in Marion's work. Being placed, it seems, bears some important relation to being conditioned. Therefore metaphysics and onto-theology, which err by thinking God in terms of prior categories and/or discourse, may be criticized for trying to give God a place. On Marion's reading, Nietzsche's philosophy makes it possible to place "the divine" somewhere utterly empty, utterly passive, utterly evacuated and yielding. As mentioned above, Marion does not find this satisfactory. It is still, after all, some kind of placing; Nietzschean "distance" ends up positing the divine as a function of the will to power for which the passive "place of the divine" stands as a perfect and necessary foil. Nevertheless, Marion does give Nietzsche credit for at least "transgress[ing] the idolatrous relation to the divine"[28] through this very freeing-up of space. One might say that, for Marion, there is a moment in Nietzsche—after the idols are smashed and the gaping emptiness begins to open, but before the will to power obligingly enters the fray as the new figure of divinity—when onto-theology is genuinely threatened. This is the "plunge into darkness" which "attest[s] to, and equally conceal[s], [Nietzsche's] sole authentic deviation from metaphysics."[29]

In the Hölderlin essay, "The Withdrawal of the Divine and the Face of the Father," this trend continues. Idolatry goes hand in hand with having a place, even a place of utter emptiness, for the divine. Furthermore, to the extent that such a place is denied—by being qualified, underdetermined, undefined, emptied, erased, etc.—one succeeds in transgressing against metaphysics. Thus as we have seen, and as Marion recalls in "Interlude 1," Nietzschean distance deviated from metaphysics in that "the divine presents itself only in its very vanishing." However, since Nietzsche allows "the metaphysical place of the supreme Being [to] persist," this vanishing is idolatrously overcome. In the form of will to power, "the divine, through a passionate return, demands the immediate assumption of the divine *persona* by man".[30] Perhaps, Marion entertains, the poetic distance of

28. Ibid.
29. Ibid.
30. Ibid., 79.

The Place of the Spirit

Hölderlin would fare better—Hölderlin, who "knew, before Nietzsche, if in a profound familiarity with him," that an alternative existed to the passionate return of the divine. According to Marion, Hölderlin dared "to think an unthinkable paradox the intimacy of man with the divine *grows* with the gap that distinguishes them," and therefore that "[t]he withdrawal of the divine would perhaps constitute its ultimate form of revelation."[31]

Marion makes this case through a lengthy exegesis of two of Hölderlin's poems, "In Lovely Blue" and "Patmos," with other exegetical stops along the way. Like Nietzsche, Hölderlin perceives that the attempt to grasp, to draw near, to the divine—here, "the Celestials."[32]—makes the divine disappear, once it is realized that what can be grasped is not divine. Unlike Nietzsche, who rushes to put an idealized humanity in the place once held by the divine, Hölderlin sees, in the divine's very withdrawal, his own exposure to a true God who draws near only in absence. Through this move, Marion suggests, Hölderlin "learn[s] from Greece how to leave Greece,"[33] a departure signaled by the realization that "the most touching proximity of the God teaches us that to move away from him—to take one's distances—is what can be done by the highest faithfulness."[34]

It is at this point, according to Marion, that Hölderlin's meditations become christological rather than celestial. As evidence Marion cites various poems contemporaneous to "Patmos" which also contain christological themes, and of which he offers a "synoptic reading."[35] These poems, according to Marion, reveal a Christ whose relationship of "irreducible"[36] distance from the Father allows the full measure of the Father's self-gift to be truly given. This is not, in other words, the Nietzschean distance which too quickly gets filled in by a new kind of divinity, by some quantity which has been sized to fit the empty space left behind by the departed idols. To the contrary, the distance between the Father and Christ exceeds and forbids any sort of recuperation or quantification; it has no dimensions, no wider horizon against which, and in terms of which, it may be measured. It is this distance that permits "proximity"[37]—permitting Christ to draw

---

31. Ibid., 80.
32. Ibid., 87.
33. Ibid., 103.
34. Ibid., 104.
35. Ibid., 105.
36. Ibid., 104
37. Ibid.

near enough to receive the gift without drawing too close and grasping it, and without being destroyed by its superabundance. Christ, in turn, freely returns the gift back to the Father—again, across distance, drawing near without grasping. To human creatures, the inexhaustibility of the Father's self-gift is revealed precisely by the fact that the human Christ does not bear it in himself. Rather, Christ "strip[s] himself of it," and through this stripping testifies to the mode of his own divinity his receptive sonship vis-à-vis the Father.[38]

In what sort of a place does this christological manifestation occur? Or, to ask another way, where does Hölderlin go, figuratively speaking, after leaving Greece? The answer is the title of the poem under consideration, as well as the site of John's apocalyptic vision Patmos. Marion's description of Patmos deserves to be quoted at length

> Why does Patmos allow approach? It does not allow it so much as it gives rise to it "poor," it can let itself be approached by "the stranger" without disfiguring him with a stateless munificence. . . . Why so "full of welcome" in its poverty? Precisely because poor. Patmos prepares the space in which the god neither obfuscates man with its presence nor, as in the henceforth "atheistic" Greece, saddens man with its absence.[39]

By comparing these two poems, Marion sets up Patmos (in all its senses) as a placial counterpart to the "Lovely Blue," the background against which the celestial divine is made (in Hölderlin's words) "openly manifest."[40] Patmos, with its poverty, can never serve as a divine backdrop; its poverty consists in the fact that it never becomes the place of the divine. To be encountered by God on Mt. Patmos is not the same as to encounter God on Mt. Olympus. On Patmos, God is not *here*. Patmos, rather, is a metaphor of finitude—of the creature's unbridgeable ontological distance from God. Finitude marks God's withdrawal from creation (for finitude could never contain or grasp God), but finitude is also the creature's very being, given freely from God. Thus, on Patmos one receives one's being—is encountered by—a God who is not there. Patmos is thus both placed and poor, and for one and the same reason because it is contingent, contained, inscribed from without by the God whose cannot be inscribed and is therefore far off. On Patmos, as in the desert (to cite another placial image Marion uses)

38. Ibid., 111.
39. Ibid., 104–5.
40. Ibid., 89.

The Place of the Spirit

"every idolatrous form disappears"[41] and nothing comes in to take its place, leaving it poor.

It is important to note, at this point, what Marion has not said. He has not posited a general rule of an inverse relationship, such that the *less* placially determined a horizon is, the *more* appropriate it will be for God. But it does seem that Marion points out, on more than one occasion, the dangers associated with giving God a place—and thus raises the possibility that any God who shows up in a "place of the divine" is a God sized-to-fit. Patmos designates that place where this does not happen, because God stands at a distance which is marked christologically. Patmos' "poverty" contains an implicit admission that it cannot contain, and therefore it ends up being the place where God truly encounters. But is *God* in any sense placed in the encounter? God is not placed *by Patmos*. That much is clear. But does Patmos, in a sense, stand for all possible placing, in the same way that it stands for creaturely finitude? Does God's withdrawal from Patmos—God's encountering from across a distance—mean that God is in no sense placed?

In fact there would be problems if Marion were to say something like this, that God is no sense placed. He makes this clear in the final essay in *Idol and Distance*, which I shall treat only briefly. In "The Distance of the Requisite and the Discourse of Praise Denys" Marion reflects upon the possibility for non-idolatrous discourse about God, taking his cues from Denys' "The Divine Names." Speaking about God is, Marion makes clear, a tricky business if one is to avoid idolatry. To straightforwardly predicate anything of God—even something as simple as "God is good"—seems on the face of it to situate God with reference to a wider horizon of goodness. A striking feature of Marion's christology, in the Denys essay, is the importance it attaches to the divine Name, in which God gives what is unthinkable in the thinkable. Historically given first in the tetragrammaton, the Name refuses predication—refuses naming—for God has not crossed distance and given God's name in order to be grasped as an object. But the Name is without any suitable language (it is still the unspeakable Name of God) until the incarnation, death and resurrection of Christ. Then Christ—the divine Word—is "humanized through incarnation and glorified through resurrection," and receives the unspeakable Name of the Father. Since, as divine Word, Christ is "saying itself," the Name is given over to be said; and since Christ is humanized, humans may speak the Name in "homology" with

---

41. Ibid., 124–25.

Christ.[42] Even so, mere predicative discourse still will not suit. Discourse must be, and is, broken open and made capable of a non-predicative speaking of the divine Name praise. This breaking open of language happens, moreover, after the manner of a death. As Christ, the divine Word, dies and is resurrected, so too predicative discourse dies in the apophatic moment and is resurrected into praise.[43] Praise, then—and not simple negation—is the way to speak non-idolatrously about God. To simply deny things of God—to deny things of God in a way that is "only an inversion of the category" of predication[44]—is vulnerable to idolatry as well; for "[i]n place of saying what God is, it would say what God is not" and therefore "remains idolatrous."[45]

The issue of negation, of course, raises the question of whether Marion does or can that God is placed, and to what degree. As I see it, at this point there are two possibilities. They are not mutually contradictory, although the first does leave open more possibilities than the second.

(1) Being placed within a horizon, and being contingent, are two aspects of one and the same reality. That is to say, both aspects signal the gift of finite being itself. This is not a negative view of place, any more than contingency itself is negative. For Marion, finitude is a freely given gift from God that admits distance from and proximity to God; indeed, it is creaturely being itself. Be that as it may, if this is what Marion means, it makes the question of *God's* placing a very tricky one. If "the place of God" were to be strictly parallel with, say, the Name of God as discussed in the Denys essay, then that would mean the following God is not found within any wider horizon, any more than God is captured by God's name. Names, horizons, concepts—all of these are subject to God's utter priority and exceeded by God's relentless superabundance. However—and this is a major stipulation—just as we, so to speak, get God's Name back christologically, so too do we get God's place back christologically. In other words, Marion could be saying something like this From the standpoint of created place, a God who is not conditioned by any horizon looks to be no-*where*. However, distance—the very same distance that allows the gift of finite, placed being—is incarnate in Christ. Christ, the human Christ, was of course placed. The "placing" of Christ in the incarnation overflows from the Father's self-gift

42. Ibid., 144.
43. Ibid., 142–44.
44. Ibid., 147.
45. Ibid.

of the Son which truly gives the Son a place vis-à-vis the Father. In other words, paternal-filial distance must truly "place" the Son. It cannot make the Son all situating by refusing to place him. Therefore, just as, in Christ, we have truly been given God's Name, so have we been given God's place, because Christ was placed in the incarnation. To try and, in a sense, "get behind" the filial gift—so as to find some *more real* place against which God shows up—is to overreach, to transgress against distance, and lapse into idolatry.

(2) But there is a second possibility—one that contains both more and less reserve than the first. In this scenario, Marion is more hesitant to give God any kind of real placing, so implicated is place in idolatry. Yet he is less hesitant to negate something of God—denying, precisely, that God is placed. Here, *refusal* of placing is, on some level, a *necessary* part of God's priority and superabundance. In the first of these two possibilities one can read Marion as stopping with Christ and looking no further. Here, however, Marion might be said to peek under the christological curtain and straightforwardly deny placing of God. Crucially—and this was my point in bringing up the Denys essay—such a denial of placing would seem to be a categorical negation; God is categorically *not* placed. Given what Marion has said about categorical negations, such a reading, if it were correct, would raise questions about whether Marion has broken one of his own rules. Furthermore, if this interpretation is correct we do not get place back in the end (in the way that we get back the Name, for example) for place is implicated in idolatry itself. There can be no question of any real placing to paternal-filial distance the whole point of distance, here, is exactly to deny placing, to mow down any boundaries that would presume to contain it or put conditions upon it. The place of distance is no-place.

Put this way, it seems to me that the first scenario coheres much better with Marion's wider project. But is it what he actually says? By way of evidence for the second reading, we have multiple instances where placiality is closely associated with idolatry, not to mention the fact that the incarnated Christ's actual, lived placial reality—his life in first century Palestine—is not central. On the other hand, the placial status of Patmos vis-à-vis God, and more importantly the placing of the Son via the Father, is ambiguous. With respect to *Idol and Distance* I think one could argue for either interpretation. When one moves on to *Prolegomena to Charity* and *God Without Being*, I think, one finds a great deal more evidence for the second interpretation. In particular, in parts of *Prolegomena to Charity*, placing takes on a more negative connotation, and not only in conjunction with idolatry. Second, Marion's trinitarian theology reproduces the problem but in a trinitarian context, where yet more problems emerge. Paternal-filial distance—in the person of the Son—is and must be so all determining, so without containment or qualification, that the Son exhausts all the possibilities for any kind of distance from (and therefore proximity to) the Father. Accordingly, the Father becomes the trinitarian person of whom placing is necessarily (and therefore categorically) denied. The Spirit, in turn, has no trinitarian "place" to appear at all, and ends up being reduced to a qualifier or power of Christ. These observations, if true, would seem to tip the scale in favor of interpretation number two. That is the case I shall try to make in the next section.

Eucharistic and Trinitarian Sites?

In this section I shall consider whether the Eucharistic and trinitarian "sites" of theology—which function similarly in *Prolegomena to Charity* and *Idol and Distance*—in fact return place christologically. In other words, I want to see whether Marion holds that place, with all that it smacks of idolatry, can—like the Name, the concept, etc.—be recuperated once paternal-filial distance is respected. It seems clear to me that this is what Marion intends; the Eucharistic and trinitarian sites, Marion will say, give creation the space to return christologically back to the Father in the Spirit. As such, they are set up as a non-idolatrous placing—to be distinguished from an idolatrous placing wherein the divine shows up in measure to a set of preconditions. But does Eucharistic/trinitarian placing, as Marion lays them out. really redeem place in this fashion? There are a number of factors to consider.

The most important consideration may be that, apart from his discussion of Eucharistic and trinitarian sites, Marion's evaluations of place are somewhat more decisive *Prolegomena to Charity* and *God Without Being* than they were in *The Idol and Distance*. Of the two possible readings of Marion I offered, above, these texts tend to support the second that the only non-idolatrous placing appropriate to God is an outright *refusal* to be placed, which refusal looks like distance to placed creatures such as ourselves, and which refusal mirrors Christ's refusal of placing. (The alternative, again, would be a reading of Marion wherein christological placing is understood in a more positive sense, such that Christ is positively—if ineffably—placed *as divine*, which placing grounds his being located in the incarnation.)

The Place of the Spirit

It is not that Marion radically revises his argument. Early in *God Without Being*, for example, Marion covers old ground by arguing that "[o]nto-theo-logy disengages, of itself a function and hence a site for every intervention of the divine that would be constituted as metaphysical the theo-logical pole of metaphysics determines . . . a site for what one later names 'God.'"[46] Here, as in *Idol and Distance*, Marion is allergic to place being predicated in any sense of God, inasmuch as place tends to stand for contingency. In *Prolegomena to Charity* and *God Without Being* the urgency of Marion's worry appears, to me, to support the second interpretation. In the essay in *Prolegomena to Charity* entitled "The Intentionality of Love," for example, Marion's suspicions about place extend not only to *God's* placing, but to the placing of any other. He has Heidegger in his sights, of course. Even in *Idol and Distance* Marion is critical—implicitly and explicitly—of Heidegger's prizing of place. Marion does not see that renewed focus on Dasein's practical life will offer any help in terms of a way out of idolatry. In a section in which Marion addresses Heidegger specifically, he writes

> [T]he worshipper . . . knows himself to be the artisan who has worked with metal, wood, or stones to the point of offering the god and image to be seen . . . so that the god should consent to take on a face in it. . . . What, then, does the worshipper worship in the idol? . . . [W]hat man, in the city or community, experiences as divine, as the divinity that precedes any face and any image . . .[47]

The tools of Dasein's practical life that had so charmed Heidegger—tools for working with metal, wood, and stones—are just as capable of fixing God and making God present, suggests Marion, as are the conceptual tools of philosophy. Indeed, the fact that this discussion precedes the discussion of metaphysics, suggests that Marion is making a stronger point that what Heidegger had posited as a remedy, was in fact more of the same.

However, in *Idol and Distance*, Marion's critique of Heidegger is not an explicitly Levinasian one. In "The Intentionality of Love," by contrast, Marion's suspicions about place are expressed within a Levinasian meditation upon the phenomenology of the other. For Levinas, Heidegger's attachment to place evinces the latter's "very scission of humankind into natives and strangers." Heidegger, from the start preoccupied with Being at the expense of ethics, was content to rail against any number of culprits in modernity; yet all of them, according to Levinas, were "less dangerous

---

46. Marion, *God without Being*, 34.
47. Marion, *Idol and Distance*, 5.

than the ghosts of the Place."[48] Levinas sees all of Heidegger's seemingly innocuous spatial and placial concepts—room, dwelling, clearing—as made possible by the reduction of the Other to the same, under the guise of ontology. The reduction is made possible by the "interposition of a middle and neutral term," an area in which I egoistically encounter the Other as an object. To avoid such egoism, Levinas argues, one must be "[f]reed from all holy abodes" so that one "can discover the authentic meaning of the human way of being in the world: we are here in order to provide food and shelter for the Others,"[49] whether stranger or native.

In "The Intentionality of Love," Marion rehearses many of Levinas' critique of Heidegger. Exteriority, in particular, functions in this essay as a figure of alterity, of "objects transcendent and exterior to" a consciousness that inevitably refers to objects outside itself.[50] Elsewhere Marion likens alterity to a horizon; the Other, he says, oversteps my autistic love "like the horizon whose line recedes in proportion as one draws near to it."[51] What is striking, though, is the way that both of these placial metaphors imply a kind of flight from location itself. Here exteriority is ever departing from the "within" of my consciousness; the horizon, meanwhile, recedes ever further the closer I approach. Later in the essay the image of the pupil—though not as obviously placial—performs a similar function. Namely, the pupil pinpoints that of the Other which refuses to be located by my gaze. The language Marion uses to describe the pupil reminds one of the images of desolation and emptiness which had earlier characterized the place of the divine. In "this ever black point," he writes, "in the very midst of the visible, there is nothing to see, except an invisible and untargetable void."[52]

In fact, throughout the essay, the only instances where Marion speaks of inclusion-within, rather than evacuation-without, show up in discussions of visibility. And in this meditation, visibility carries a decidedly negative connotation. For the Other to show up as "visible" I must reduce the Other to an object, thereby disqualifying her or him as Other.[53] "Only the object," Marion writes, "is visible, and the entrance into visibility qualifies an object

---

48. Levinas, "Heidegger, Gagarin, and Us," in Lévinas, *Difficult Freedom*, 232.
49. Ibid., 233.
50. Marion, *Prolegomena to Charity*, 72.
51. Ibid., 81.
52. Ibid.
53. Ibid., 80.

as such."[54] To be thoroughly located—to show up, visibly, *in* the gaze—is to be objectified. By contrast, to look upon an other as Other, one must look with the "invisible gaze," which centers on the "untargetable void" of the pupil. Further, the *crossing* of the "invisible gaze"—the closest thing to a "place" where this encounter with the other may be said to occur—actually occurs no-where.

Overall, in this essay of Marion's, there seems to be a heightened urgency regarding an outright *refusal* of placing. It is one thing to say that an Other, or God, cannot exhaustively be located with respect to myself, or with respect to a prior horizon. It is another to say that, in order for distance to remain intact, the gaze must be disturbed by something abyssal, empty, and untargetable—*where such modifiers are understood as opposed to placing, and therefore in a sense "place" the refusal of placing.* That, I think, is what is going on here—albeit not in an explicitly trinitarian vein—in "The Intentionality of Love." I further believe that these same tendencies are also given theological expression in "The Gift of a Presence" (in *Prolegomena to Charity*) and in "The Eucharistic Site of Theology" (in *God Without Being*). This is where Marion ostensibly returns place to us—that is, place as conditioned by christology, rather than the other way around. However, as I read Marion, it seems that what Marion actually gives us are "sites" for theology that place only the refusal of place. Place, in other words, ends up not being given; rather, what is accomplished is a successful dislocation. In order to defend these claims, I shall first try to explain what Marion means by both "trinitarian site" and "eucharistic site." Then I shall explain why Marion's most in-depth discussions of paternal-filial distance require these sites to refuse place.

In the essay in *Prolegomena to Charity* entitled "The Gift of a Presence," Marion reflects upon the gospel accounts of Christ's ascension—and, specifically, upon the manner in which Christ's physical disappearance makes possible his Eucharistic presence, which in turn provides his disciples with a Eucharistic "site" from which to "become . . . Christs" and ascend to the Father as Christ did.[55] The "site" is, not surprisingly, figured in terms of distance this time, the distance between Christ and his disciples, made possible by Christ's departure from them. Having returned, across distance, as the only begotten Son to the self-giving Father, Christ's glory

54. Ibid.
55. Ibid., 142.

was more than the disciples could bear.[56] The "disappearance at Emmaus" makes possible a new kind of presence, one bearable to them and "if it dare be said, *more real* still than this physical presence of Christ" but dependent upon his withdrawal.[57] Had Christ remained on earth he would have made God "too close"—too vulnerable to being caught in the disciples' gaze as an object, or else dazzling them with a glory that would destroy them. Instead, Christ withdraws while remaining present—at a distance. This distance is measured in the eucharist, the mode of Christ's presence that begins once his fleshly body has departed. This is what Marion calls Christ's "negative act" of "taking distance in relation to us."[58] One should note the way in which Marion considers Christ's Eucharistic presence as practically an improvement upon—"more real" than—the mode of presence during Christ's earthly life (or, presumably, the post-resurrection appearances). "For Christ," he writes, "even in the flesh, remains for them an individual, other, distinct, separate, who can 'draw near' . . . to 'walk with' them."[59] Christ's fleshly body is not a communicable gift, Marion asserts tellingly, because "bodies do not unite, they separate[.]" The Eucharistic body, by contrast, "assimilates to itself those who assimilate it . . . [and] makes itself a gift communicable to the point of assimilation."[60]

And what is the role of the Holy Spirit in this new mode of presence? This is, after all, an essay that touches upon such pneumatologically ripe themes as the church, the resurrection, the ascension, and the eucharist; yet the Holy Spirit hardly shows up as a distinct person. In fact, there are only two ways in which the Holy Spirit shows up at all first, as the power of Christ to be eucharistically present to the disciples without overwhelming them; and second, as the power of the disciples to act in a christic manner. Although I have listed these separately, for Marion they are both sides of the same *christological* coin. Thus Marion writes that one of the "conditions" that must be met in order for the disciples to assume their trinitarian site, is that "the disciples have in their heart the strength to perform their role, as well as in mind the 'spirit' of what they will perform."[61] This strength

---

56. "[T]he disappearance at Emmaus hides from the eyes of the disciples an unbearable glory" (Marion, *Prolegomena to Charity*, 136).

57. Ibid.

58. Ibid., 142.

59. Ibid., 136.

60. Ibid.

61. Ibid., 142.

is given by virtue of the fact that "Christ has introduced the trinitarian play into the world" by "perform[ing] the trinitarian gesture from the depths of humanity, from sin and thus from death."[62] This gesture, in turn, is what makes possible the sending of the Spirit; the fact that Christ, "by his departure toward the Father and across death," has "reconquer[ed] the Spirit" for his disciples. Thus one begins to see here that, for Marion, pneumatology is figured christologically, as well it should be, but the opposite is not the case. Christ's work situates the sending of the Spirit—indeed, is cast in terms of a "reconquering" of the Spirit—but there is no correlative situating of christology by pneumatology.

Further, although Marion does not say so outright, his notions of assimilation seem to require that Christ move from being placed (in his fleshly body) to *not* being placed (in his eucharistic body) in order for the disciples to be assimilated eucharistically. As long as Christ and the disciples are placed within a horizon together, his thinking seems to be, they are somewhat paradoxically divided by being too close; they cannot become assimilated into a Christ whom they perceive as an object, and Christ could assimilate them without overstepping ontological distance and destroying them with his glory. Therefore Christ has to be, in a sense, transposed from a local presence to a dislocated, deferring presence in the eucharist in order for the assimilation to occur.

The same could be said about another similar recuperation of place—where Marion discusses the "eucharistic site of theology" in an essay by the same name in *God Without Being*. This chapter of *God Without Being* reproduces many of the same central insights found in "The Gift of a Presence." The focus, though, is different; here Marion considers placing specifically in relation to discourse. If the central question of the Denys essay in *Idol and Distance* was, "How may one speak about God," then here the central question is something like, "From what vantage point—what placing—is it possible to speak about God?" Marion's answer—from a "eucharistic site"—is in many ways just an extension of what he had earlier said in "The Gift of a Presence," but with a closer focus on Christ as the divine Word and the placing of discourse in relation to this Word. Revisiting the themes of the earlier text, Marion writes, "the theologian finds his place in the Eucharist because the Eucharist itself . . . offers itself as place."[63] Here as before, the eucharistic presence of Christ, through its very deferral, seems

---

62. Ibid., 143.
63. Marion, *God without Being*, 153.

to make possible a locus from which finitude may be assimilated to Christ without being consumed by his glory, and without claiming to grasp. Here, though, the finitude in question is precisely discourse, and thus in Christ the "place . . . is opened for an absolute hermeneutic, a *theology*."[64]

It is very instructive to note the kind of placing that that the divine Word is required to do, and required *not* to do, in relation to the Father. Across distance, the Word "receives from the Father the mandate and the injunction . . . to say," that is, to manifest the gift that the Father has given in begetting. This gift is not other than distance. However, *what* the Word speaks *is also distance*, that is to say, "the message already coincides otherwise (or precisely not otherwise) with that message which the paternal illocution eternally realizes in him as Word."[65] The fact is, both of these christological sites—the site from which the disciples (and therefore the church) may be assimilated into Christ and return to the Father; and the site from which Christian discourse may be assimilated into the divine Word in praise of the Father—make Christ into the horizon for relation to the Father. Paternal-filial distance, in other words, is not placed, nor can it be. Rather, it becomes the horizon that must refuse placing *so as to* trump any other horizon. Therefore the sites that Marion offers—sites intended to be a christological recuperation of place—seem to me to have a very strange status. On the one hand, as horizon for relation to the Father, Christ "places" the disciples, the Word "places" Christian discourse. This emplacement is what is supposed to make possible Christian charity—the love necessary for Christians to make disciples of "all the nations," without "sink[ing] into ambient raving imperialism" or "fall[ing] back into the most nationalistic political messianism."[66]

However, it is hard to see any christological grounding for being placed, and hence for the placedness of creation. Why is creation placed? The Son is not placed vis-à-vis the Father, but is the horizon for a placed creation. Where does being placed enter the picture? Between begetting and creation? And if so, how?

---

64. Ibid., 151.
65. Ibid., 142.
66. Marion, *Prolegomena to Charity*, 149.

Marion's Contribution to a Trinitarian Theology of Place

As I see it the issue boils down to this is distance—in all the keys in which it sounds in Marion's theological symphony—a kind of placing, or a refusal of placing? Earlier I suggested that Marion can be read either way in *The Idol and Distance*. Although he is anxious to avoid a kind of idolatrous placing—wherein the divine fills a place determined for it by prior conditions—Marion does not yet, it seems to me, categorically deny that God is placed by strongly asserting that Christ is the only horizon. I have also suggested that one sees a hardening of his position in *Prolegomena to Charity* and *God Without Being*, even while he makes more of an effort to offer christological "sites" in exchange for the idolatrous horizons he has taken away. By way of evidence we have the Levinasian arguments in "The Intentionality of Love," lines of thought that Levinas himself did develop as a refusal of Heidegger's prizing of place. We also have the moves Marion makes in "The Gift of a Presence" and "On the Eucharistic Site of Theology," in which, it seems, christological presence must become dislocated in order to be the horizon for these two sites. Earlier I offered two possible interpretations of Marion—one in which he did not categorically negate God's placiality, and one in which he did. If the first were the case, I suggested, we would discover that paternal-filial distance does truly "place" the Son. However, if I am correct, paternal-filial distance actually displaces the Son so as to make him all situating, so as to make possible a "site" for the encounter of created being and God.

In my opinion, this problem turns out to be central to Marion's understanding of how filial distance operates. The Father's self-gift in love, the Son, and the withdrawal of the Father that admits relation—these are not three different aspects of Marion's theology. "Paternal distance" names all of these. The Son, Marion is clear, does not stand at one pole of some kind of intra-divine clearing, with the Father at the other. I believe he is right to so insist, for reasons I have discussed in the previous chapter. However, the way that Marion avoids the pitfall of an intra-divine clearing, is to say that all horizons for relation to the Father are exhausted by and in the Son. This is the flipside of one of the main strengths of Marion's project: his ability to catch everything—discourse, concepts, being, etc.—in the same christological net.

Thus, the chief problem I see in Marion's project is not that he may have committed a categorical negation and thus risked self-contradiction.

Nor is it even that it is difficult to find any christological grounding for being placed, if Christ is the all-locating horizon. The most foundational problem has to do with pneumatology. If the Holy Spirit is a divine Person—and therefore, one presumes, cannot be caught up in the christological net, at least not in the same way as the rest of creation—then Marion's theology of filial distance causes problems. There is some kind of trinitarian relation that is not identical to filiation; yet this does not seem to be allowed in Marion's theology. And, in fact, Marion *does* tend to situate the Holy Spirit within the christological horizon. How, then, can one retain Marion's central theological insights, while making a place for the Spirit—and for place itself? How, for that matter, can we judiciously retain the positive characteristics of all of the placial and trinitarian models thus far considered, while avoiding some of the pitfalls?

A complete constructive treatment will have to be postponed until a subsequent book; but in the chapter that follows I shall give an example of how such a trinitarian theology of place might proceed.

5

Notes Toward a Trinitarian Theology of Place

Beginnings of a Synthesis

ALL THE INTERLOCUTORS ARE NOW ASSEMBLED. ALTHOUGH THIS IS THE final chapter, I see it as the beginning of the task at hand, which is to think more systematically about how categories of space and place bear upon the Christian doctrine of the trinity and the tradition of theological reflection it has yielded.

In the sole chapter that remains I will not give an exhaustive answer to such a broad question. I will not construct a fully fleshed-out systematic theology of trinity and location in the space of one chapter. I will, however, give an example of how the question might take shape if my assembled experts are allowed to illuminate and inform each other's work. In so doing, I hope to show that a theological consideration of trinity and space/place will have to contend, centrally, with pneumatology.

Some of the insights will come from the Cappadocians and Augustine, who to a person insist that any understanding of God's location must evade the obvious folly of simple delimitation—just as any finite creature's inquiry about God must evade the folly of capturing God within a concept. I do think it likely that Augustine structures the relationship between place and knowledge a bit differently than do Basil and the Gregories. As I suggested previously, this difference strikes me as one of sensibility and cadence. For the purposes of this dissertation, however, the more salient detail lies in a point of symmetry between the two. In both instances, a shift in perspective happens when we ask after God's location vis-à-vis human knowledge. In the Cappadocians' case, to generalize, the shift involves our discovery that we (and our discursive knowledge) have our own perimeter, given us by the triune God. For Augustine, if we try to generate a concept of God inside our minds, we find (or should find) that we are created and known by a triune God who has given us minds, and to whom intelligibility itself testifies. From both, one can extrapolate a theological maneuver to use as the basis for a trinitarian theology of place: In trying to place God we discover we are placed. Thus "place" falls squarely on the created side, but without being so opposed to God that one is forced to argue strongly for a God who is placially outside of place.

I take this shift to be necessary starting point for a trinitarian theology of location. Does Marion then win the day, in my view, inasmuch as he also advocates a very emphatic sort of perspectival reversal? Has he taken the best insights of the fathers and brought them up to current code? Let me say, first, that I think Marion's three early works show us a great deal about what a trinitarian theology of place needs to accomplish. In the end, though, I do not think that Marion exactly gets place right. Nor do I think that Moltmann exactly gets place right; although he, more than Marion, shows us what a trinitarian theology of place can and ought to accomplish. In fact, very often, the points missed by Moltmann turn out to be the points grasped by Marion and vice versa. If they hold a fault in common, it is this: both are overly inclined to ask place to do theological work that does not suit it. In Marion's case, place and space get no traction of their own. Place and space, rather, stand as figures for all idolatrous horizons—but Being and conceptual thought most centrally. By contrast, for Moltmann, his best placial and spatial insights are prevented from doing all that they might, lest they intrude upon or qualify his dialectical structure.

These problematic elements can be corrected by a judicious application of the work of the placial theorists of chapter one, as well as the patristic thinkers from chapter two. Heidegger and Bachelard, as discussed, have Descartes in their sights, and specifically the Cartesian *res extensa*. They, as well as Tuan, critique Descartes not simply by offering a better account of domains, but by drawing attention to how human perspectives actually confer place upon the world by structuring it, navigating within it, imbuing it with meaning, and trying to understand it. And here is where the placial theorists of chapter one and the late ancient thinkers of chapter two will find an odd sort of common cause. Some of the placial and spatial influences upon the Cappadocians and Augustine were at least generally Neo-Platonist—with more concentrated doses in some authors and works,

The Place of the Spirit

and more dilute versions in others. I am intentionally leaving open the question of exactly what placial notions came specifically to which church father from (for example) Plotinus versus Iamblichus, and which placial notions were simply in the philosophical and cultural reservoir. While that inquiry could be very fruitful, I lack the space to do it justice here. I therefore have made the much more modest claim—following Ed Casey—that Neo-Platonism in general took into account Stoic, Epicurean, and Atomist models of place and space "while always addressing themselves explicitly to Plato and even more especially to Aristotle."[1] The attempt to harmonize, to take into account multiple conceptions of space and place, resulted (according to Casey) in two characteristically Neo-Platonist innovations: first, the addition of more possible kinds of place; and second, the stipulation that the *less* material sorts of place are in fact the more powerful ones.

I do not think this is altogether foreign to the way in which Father, Son and Spirit gets placially marked in Basil, Nyssen, Nazianzen and Augustine. To be sure, they insert various important hedges against emanationism—the most fundamental of which, for the present purpose, is the reversal just mentioned. But I do see, in the patristic trinitarian theologies under consideration here, a willingness to imagine placiality anew. When the patristic interlocutors wrestle with the problem of where God is vis-à-vis creation—where, so to speak, God's placial coverage stops and creation's placial coverage starts—they carefully attend to the problems inherent in asking the question in this fashion. But they do not, in so doing, obliterate the possibility of talking about God in placial terms, nor in giving created place some sort of theological grounding connected to the trinitarian economy. It boils down to a choice: Do we reckon our own spatial and conceptual limits according to our faith in a God who fills all things? Or do we (falsely) plot God's limits according to a human spatial and conceptual calculus that believes itself to be unlimited in its proper scope? To choose the former is not to abrogate place—let alone to say that the most fundamental thing about God is that God is not here. In fact there is a way to talk about place and the trinity, in the theological economy, and with the appropriate qualifications.

Somewhat surprisingly, modern and postmodern retrievals of place (of the sort discussed in chapter one) help expose these patristic insights and render them systematically useful today. Together, these two clusters of thought—patristic trinitarian thought on the one hand, and modern/

---

1. Casey, *Fate of Place*, 88.

postmodern reflection on place and space on the other—suggest non-volumetric ways of imagining inner and outer, expansiveness and delimitation, power and room and coinherence. All of these are theologically useful. Moltmann grasps them and uses them; Marion less so. But when it comes to envisioning place under the aspect of intelligibility, even Moltmann does not follow. Ultimately, moments within Moltmann's theology require space to be a domain whose spatiality is both prior, and required for a dialectical process. Likewise, logic of Marion's paternal distance assumes place and space as stand-ins for all domains. The unique aspect of Marion's thought is that God's distance refuses domains so entirely. In order to avoid being conditioned by human horizons, Marion affirms, God must be both elsewhere and no-place. Consequently all domains are abrogated by God, but it is very clearly domains which are abrogated. For Moltmann it tends to work in rather the opposite direction. In order to have God here with us—and perhaps more to the point, in order to meaningfully connect a doctrine of God with a concern for ecology—we must be able to come up with domains which coinhere. Thus the trinity becomes, in Moltmann's later work, a "broad place" that perichoretically coinheres with the domain of creation.

In sum, then, I am using this final chapter to tell a very particular story about place, space, trinity, and the possibility for theology. In antiquity—so my story goes—there was no pressing reason for an understanding of place with nearly the existential, psychological, and humanistic elements such as we find in Heidegger, Bachelard, and Tuan. There would have been no direct antecedent for such an understanding, no problematizing of human subjectivity and experience that would have pressed the issue in the same way that it was pressed in modernity. While not laying blame, I nevertheless find compelling theological reasons to marry certain placial elements of patristic trinitarian thought, with the broadened definition of place offered by the later placial theorists. The theological synthesis I am envisioning runs thus: In the economy, from the standpoint of human creatures, we encounter God in a manner which we perceive to involve navigability, roominess, locatedness, the coinherence of inner and outer, and an interplay of beholding and constructing. Place—I suggest, following Bachelard, Heidegger, and Tuan—legitimately involves all of these things. But God—as we learn from both the Cappadocians and Augustine—is not exhaustively subject to our ways of plotting and navigating. To the contrary, we are placed by God. Therefore, the reality often referred to in theological shorthand as "the economic trinity" actually grounds what creatures experience place

. . . of which strict extension and delimitation make up only one small aspect.

The need to posit an "elsewhere" for God is *also* properly placial, and required by the economy. The "divine elsewhere" in question is not a pre-constituted inaccessible arena where God exists apart from us; nor is it the infinite withdrawal of God into paternal distance; nor is it an unacceptable obstacle to having God here with us. It is simply something that must be postulated by placed creatures whose placiality derives from the triune economy. In this sense, the divine elsewhere is akin to Tuan's "mythical space." By this I do not mean to suggest that God is mythical; only that the requirement that God be put (so to speak) "somewhere other than here, located outside of place" fulfills much the function that Tuan ascribes to mythical space. Mythical space does not pick out an actual physical (or, I would add, ontological) expanse. Rather, mythical space must be postulated in order to orient ourselves; that is the purpose it serves. Such a purpose does not make it non-placial, however—for again, place includes anything having to do with navigability, orientation, inner and outer, beholding and constructing. As such, it too derives from the trinitarian economy—for place itself, including its experiential and humanistic overtones, so derives. It may be that I am trying to build a placial case analogous to the case for apophasis; so perhaps it ought not surprise either myself or the reader to find deep symmetry between the two. As with apophatic language, divine placing turns out to be more about our own createdness than about the precise delineation of deity. Recognition of one's own createdness, though, certainly provides theological content, even telling us something about who God is for us.

Patristic Interventions

For Basil, Nyssen, and Nazianzen, the mental activity of circumscription is theologically fraught—as fraught as the very question of the possibility of natural theology, to which it is so closely linked. Apprehending anything intelligible in the cosmos, whether visible or invisible, involves demarcating it, picking it out from its surroundings, and understanding it through a consonance of mind and thing. Clearly, though, this cannot work straightforwardly for God as it does for other discrete items and quantities in the cosmos. If one doubted the problem, one had only to look at the Arianism of Eunomius and his supporters, who applied to the Logos the same sort of discursive reason and mental circumscription which one would ordinarily and properly apply to creatures. By virtue of the fact that the Logos was begotten and the Father unbegotten, Eunomius claimed, one could draw two different conceptual perimeters around the two. One could circumscribe the Father with the category "unbegotten," and the Son with the category "begotten."

Such circumscription will not do, according to Basil and the Gregories, not least because it introduced an interval—and hence distention, alienation, and contingency—into the godhead (as discussed at length in chapter two). But Eunomianism was not the only theological danger with which they were contending. Even as the Cappadocians had to guard against the introduction of contingency into God, they dueled as well with the emanationist impulse of removing contingency from creation. How to get contingency to adhere fully to creation (so that it's not a necessary emanation of the One) but not at all to the godhead (so that the Son does not end up being circumscribable by virtue of being "begotten" when the Father is "unbegotten"?) And how then to affirm that the knowledge of God is still possible?

Epistemology, theological language, and place thus attach to the same basic problem in which the status of all three is called into question. The characteristically Cappadocian response, as we have seen, is a particular sort of rejoinder: the intellective tendency to circumscribe contingent quantities gets, itself, circumscribed according to an altogether different and ineffable logic. It is not, in other words, that the activity of finite minds does not get circumscribed by an even more expansive quantity which operates according to the same basic coordinates and procedures. Rather, human knowledge runs up against its *own* limit when it tries erroneously to confine God within conceptual fences. One can either perceive, correctly, that the periphery is for our side alone—in which case some knowledge about God might be possible for us. Alternately, we can erroneously position our own discursive reason as that which "fills all things" with our philosophical projections about causality, requiring even God to submit to the confines we have established.

What happens, placially and spatially, if one does proceed with an appropriately limited understanding of human knowledge? What is involved in seeking knowledge about God, not in order to falsely confine God, but in order to achieve "the goal of our calling"? And more to the point, is there *no* placially significant theological element here? What of Basil's remark

The Place of the Spirit

that "[t]he Spirit is often spoken of as the place (chora) of those who are being sanctified"[2] even as the Spirit indwells the hearts of believers? What of ascent and descent, two metaphors through which the saving processes of the divine economy are made discursively comprehensible—with God coming "down" so as to raise us "up"?

On my reading, Cappadocian theology shows the logic of discursive circumscription for what it is: finite, creaturely, and (what we in the twenty-first century are in a position to call) placial. Circumscription is not the same as corporeal extension (they counted incorporeal angels among the intelligible creatures, for example), but certainly it has everything to do with finitude and delimitation. The fact that circumscription is shown to be bounded by the God who fills all things does not mean, however, that knowledge about God can never be appropriately placial. To the contrary, God's creative and saving action seems to confer to creation something experienced by creatures as having directionality, height and depth, interiority and exteriority and a coinherence of the two, and navigability. I am here making explicit a point I glean simply from the abundance of place language in, especially, Basil's discussion of the economy of salvation. I presume to take it a bit further than what they explicitly state, and to argue positively that place—understood broadly to include all world structuring, finding, and dwelling—derives from the trinitarian economy. God fills creation; God has come (as we experience it) "down here" from "up there;" and God's Spirit is in our hearts even as we are in the Spirit. True, none of these behave in exactly the way that physical circumscription exactly behaves... but that only goes to show how derivative and partial is physical circumscription. The height, depth, aroundness, indwelling, interiority and exteriority which (from our perspective) unfailingly attend God's action towards us—these yield place and space. Thus, we need not take care at every point to emphasize God's refusal of created horizons or enclosures. Indeed, once circumscription is shown to be inultimate and contingent anyway—such that even the worrisome binary of "inner" and "outer" is destabilized in the Spirit—why go to such trouble? Particularly when placial language promises so many theological payoffs, when used properly? For again, as I read the Cappadocians, trinitarian place language will never be rooted out of discussions of the divine economy, and in fact seems uniquely suited to expressing it.

---

2. Anderson, *St. Basil the Great On the Holy Spirit*, 94; also given (with translation of "chora") in Bobrinskoy, "The Indwelling of the Spirit of Christ," 57.

Notes Toward a Trinitarian Theology of Place

In advancing this position, I have, as I say, performed an intervention—but I think it may turn out to be a rather modest one. I am including under "place" all the senses of place that the later theorists of place include. At points, such inclusion seems to run against the general tendency of Basil, Nyssen, and Nazianzen to equate place with delimitation and circumscription. But conversely, the broader definition of place seems to me to harmonize with placial language used to describe the economy of salvation. The advantage lies in how neatly it makes "place" to line up with other hallmarks of creatureliness, without thereby divorcing place from the economy. Place joins such categories as discursive knowledge, symbolic thought, history, and time—all of them, in different ways, marking that asymmetrical boundary where human existence runs up against its limit conditions; yet for this reason indicating an very arena in which God has acted toward creatures. Moreover, place includes elements of human life in which the coinherence of inner and outer, for example, are uncontroversial. This is to the good, because when we then find it theologically useful to talk about the Spirit dwelling in us even as we are in the Spirit, we need not allow has to how we are no longer talking about place. To the contrary, it should be expected that if created place derives from the trinitarian economy, that we would discover symmetry between spiritual journeys and any other sort of navigation. Such an ordering does not collapse God into place, nor does it leave place unexplained because of an a priori decision to limit place to extension. Rather, it says that to be created is to be placed; and to be placed is to navigate within a world we did not invent but spend a good deal of time conceptually constructing. Therefore, to be placed is, exactly, to be a creature within the triune God's *oikonomia*.

At this point a question leaps out. What of the (to use the theological term of art) the trinity *ad intra*? What about the three persons as they are *in se*, rather than *pro nobis*? Put differently, what does the asymmetry of the divine-human dividing line—the fact that it restricts us, but not God—allow or forbid us to say about God, or about place? As discussed in chapter two, Nazianzen and especially Nyssen use placial language to designate certain things about the three persons' relationships to each other. For Nyssen, *anakyklosis* and *periphera* evoked a rotating movement of the three persons around each other in the godhead. The shared term *prosopon* likewise connotes directionality, a turning of one's face toward another. The Johannine "in"—as found in Jesus' words "I am in the Father and the Father is in me"—was used by all three Cappadocians against Eunomius

129

The Place of the Spirit

and others who would subordinate the Son to the Father. Too, there are the many references to God's exteriority to place—references whose evident internal contradictions were not lost to the Cappadocians, and which prompted Nazianzen to admit thought's defeat with particular clarity when he asked whether God was nowhere or somewhere?

Here I think we find another startling point of fruitful connection between Cappadocian reflection on the trinity, and much later reflection on place. I have in mind specifically Tuan's insight about mythical space as one feature of spatial lore. Recall that, according to Tuan's taxonomy, mythical space serves to orient us in relation to things beyond our sphere of navigation. It is heuristic; it acts as if there were a way to get out of the world we inhabit, and then gestures toward the exit. If place (broadly speaking[3]) has to do with how we navigate and meaningfully structure a world which we seem not to have invented, then spatial lore is properly placial. But here I am doing a theological gloss which goes beyond what Tuan would claim. I have already suggested that to be placed, to be created by God, to be engaged in the task of orienting and navigating oneself in the world, and to thereby construct a spatial lore . . . all of these may be superimposed onto each other. Therefore, appeals to spatial lore are to be expected, as part of our navigation. I therefore suggest that mythical space and spatial lore are useful categories for imagining what we are doing when we gesture toward God's irreducibility to created categories. It is a placial gesture—the only kind we creatures can make—indicating that God is not reducible to our place. This is different from saying that the trinity in fact sits in some pre-constituted domain somewhere—impossibly located outside of place, in an alternate horizon which allows perfect interiority of the persons to each other. That is not how ascent and descent, *periphera* and *prosopon*, etc. are functioning (which is not to say they are unimportant). They are, famously so in the case of the Cappadocians, apophatic: indications that the three persons relate without being intervalized, face each other without being distended, etc.

In this way such placial language, properly understood, serves to bring the focus back to the economy again, and to what it means to be a creature. For all of the reasons expounded upon so ably by our Cappadocian guides, Christian theology requires that God not be collapsed into the intra-mundane set of circumscribable quantities. At the same time, we do need to

---

3. In other words, although I am speaking here of Tuan's notion of "spatial lore," I am not using "place" as used specifically by Tuan.

be able to get our theological bearings, and so we navigate. We speak of ascent and descent, indwelling, coinherence of individuated quantities; of realms of glory in which God resides; of an interiority to God inaccessible to creatures. We do this because we find ourselves in an *oikonomia* which we not only navigate (à la Tuan), but whose structure and life informs the patterns whereby we navigate (à la Bachelard). If we navigate appropriately, we attribute the very possibility of navigable creation to the trinitarian economy of creation and salvation. If we do not, we put God—and/or the three persons—into preconstituted discrete domains.

This is why framing place as *either* "that which God needs to be gotten out of" or "that which God needs to be gotten back into" creates unnecessary problems for trinitarian thought. One must ultimately place God on the far or near side of a symmetrical divide, and then explain how doing so neither makes God entirely absent nor straightforwardly and exhaustively present. By contrast, a broader, more sophisticated understanding of place—one which admits of spatial lore, the coinherence of inner and outer, the interplay of finding and structuring, etc.—gives other theological options. One is now in the position, for example, to note the sympathy between intimate human dwelling (as in Bachelard's archetypal home), being "in the Spirit," and the Spirit's indwelling in humans—as I have briefly done, above. Place no longer risks becoming a theological non sequitur, a category in no way grounded in an understanding of God yet already structuring all of creation.

But perhaps Augustine would be the more compelling test case. I suggest that the sort of placial interventions I made earlier, in Cappadocian trinitarian theology, are not any less appropriate here. By saying this I do not mean to erase all differences between the two. Rather, I submit that whatever differences there are do not serve to make either one an inappropriate springboard for a contemporary trinitarian theology of place. Did Augustine operate with an explicit understanding of place at all akin to that I have been advocating for? It seems not. Often, when Augustine considers locatedness as a topic of explicit and categorical attention, he seems primarily to have in mind some sort of extension—not necessarily corporeal extension, and likely not an infinite geometric void populated by punctuate sites. But it also seems to me that for Augustine—like Basil, Nyssen and Nazianzen—place language shows up, and helpfully so, for two reasons. First, one has after all to get some sort of cognitive access to God, not in order to lay claim to or God (though this is always a danger); but rather inasmuch as doing so is part of loving God. Second, acknowledging *this* fact involves, crucially, a rethinking of who situates whom—from the pretense of an intellect which would claim to situate God, to the recognition that one's creaturely possibilities are situated by God. Clearly this theological move has implications for theories of knowledge, ontology, and creation—but surely also, and for those very reasons, for place? Granted, in none of the primary sources are the placial aspects exactly thematized—but I can see nothing forbidding one, provided we use a definition of place more overlaid with meaning making and world-structuring than with simple extension.

Moreover, to do so means that fruitful possibilities emerge for Augustine's pneumatological between. If we stipulate that place—like human conceptual thought, language, etc.—derives from our being situated and known by God, and not the other way around, we can in fact make a great deal out of the notion of Spirit as the love between the Father and the Son. Rather than reducing the Spirit to an interval, an updated understanding of place allows us to notice the ways in which the Spirit's role evokes some of the ways in which place works for human creatures. Place, I have been arguing, has to do with beholding and structuring, with coming across an environment while also overlaying meaning onto it. Moreover, these are not really two distinct moments; one activity does not straightforwardly precede the other. Turning now to trinitarian thought, to imagine the Spirit as love between Father and Son as they behold each other—where the Son, meanwhile, has already been likened the Father's perfect self-representation—is not so far removed from such an understanding of place.

Beholding and representing and structuring, all while sharing some sort of "here" which is not spatial and is not about simple delimitation—all of these find cognates in contemporary thought about place. Which we should expect, if place has to do with human meaning making, and which faculty in turn refers to (without laying claim to) its triune creator. Understand, I am not suggesting—nor do I think Augustine could possibly be suggesting—that there is some realm somewhere, in which the Father and Son stand at opposite sides of a placial or spatial interval which is the Spirit. (Nor, for that matter, do I think he believes that Father, Son and Spirit reside somewhere as subsidiaries of an overarching horizon of divine essence which situates the three persons.[4]) Rather I am suggesting that place, as a

---

4. As I said before, I think the best way to understand stipulations about the ineffable divine essence is to say that they are gestures from within creation indicating that God's relationship to creation is not one of necessity or straightforward continuity. Sometimes

Notes Toward a Trinitarian Theology of Place

central feature of human meaning making, does not *necessarily* generate idols when it is prudently allowed to have some traction in trinitarian theology. To be sure, it is fraught; one might end up mapping God according to one's own spatial and placial coordinates. To guard against this danger, very good precedent turns out to be present in Augustine, even though he did not thematize place thus. Augustine (as well as the Cappadocians) indicate ways in which we might think of creaturely place as coming from God and reflecting who God is—and doing so, moreover, in ways that we will probably have to resign ourselves to expressing placially despite the oddity of doing so.

And were I to give myself license to do a contemporary placial gloss on Augustinian trinitarian theology, I would find myself again drawn to imagining the Spirit as something like (what creatures would call) place. The Spirit gathers and indwells believers, acts in the moment of creation, and furthermore even allows believers to see the cosmos rightly. On this last point we look again to Augustine's anti-Manichean stance—this time in *Confessions* 13, in which Augustine links the Spirit's role in creation with the Spirit's role in allowing believers to perceive the cosmos as created by a good God. But launching from *De Trinitate* we could—very tentatively, with many qualifications that we are not speaking predicatively—I think we could go so far as to liken the Spirit to a place for the Father and Son. But of course this immediately raises the very understandable worry that has already been raised with Augustine's controversial pneumatology—the worry that by making such a move the Spirit gets reduced, made derivative. Meanwhile the Father and the Son retain roles that are more like subjects with agency. To liken the Spirit to a place—does this not strip the Spirit of any real agential center? Or, conversely, might it not serve to give the Spirit too much say, too much determination, such that the Father and Son are conditioned pneumatologically in some sort of novel subordinationism?

These are compelling objections, although I think they rely overmuch on just the understanding of place that I have been trying to remove: an understanding in which place indicates passivity, contingency, and delimitation. Too, I reiterate that I am not suggesting that the Spirit *is* the place of the Father and Son in any sort of straightforward and everyday sense. Rather, I am suggesting that place cannot be a theological non sequitur; that, like symbolic thought and time and being and relationality, place

---

it is expressed placially—God is somehow outside of here—and sometimes it is expressed in terms of Being or concept.

The Place of the Spirit

ought to be thought alongside trinitarian concepts—with all of the same qualifications and provisos.

But what about the objection that such a model sacrifices the Spirit's agency? Here I think we would do well to consider the kind of activity and determining power that Gaston Bachelard ascribed to the childhood house in *The Poetics of Space*. The archetypal first home protects, shields, informs, resists, and takes on a sort of personality. It possesses depth, and in it both lives and psyches reverberate—while it likewise reverberates in the psyches and reveries of its inhabitants. Moreover, the childhood home is our first universe, and as such instructs us in how to meaningfully locate all subsequent universes and worlds we might come across. The family house can contain capacious spaces in miniature and vice versa. At the risk of being repetitive—once again, I am not meaning to plot the Spirit according to the coordinates of Gaston Bachelard, topoanalysis, and the family house. But if Bachelard is describing how place works for human creatures; and if certain hallmarks of creatureliness can indicate (however imperfectly and derivatively) something about the triune creator; then is it not worth noticing how Bachelard's account of the first home mimics some of the work which trinitarian theology is in the habit of ascribing to the Spirit. I refer to the activities of mutual indwelling, simultaneous beholding and symbolic representation thereof, and a certain kind of priority that accounts for subsequent worlds. At any rate, this goes some way toward helping us see that to use a placial metaphor for Spirit need not *necessarily* entail a demotion of the Spirit or a stripping of agency.

In sum, I recognize that there are certainly salient differences between Cappadocians and Augustine; and I do not think that any of the patristic thinkers simply gives us a fully operational trinitarian theology of place. Human symbolic thought is described using placial and spatial language, as is the economy of creation and redemption, but place is not thematized in the way I ultimately find necessary for the model I am trying to sketch. For this reason, I have had to intervene at points, categorizing place in a manner entirely anachronistic to the historical period in which the theologians wrote. Even so, I hope these interventions expose some fruitful possibilities for a doctrine of the trinity in which place is considered explicitly, as a facet of human symbolic and conceptual thought. Moreover, attending to the placial aspects of these trinitarian models gives a contemporary reader new ways of considering the ostensible differences—whether they exist, and what they are—between Cappadocian and Augustinian trinitarian thought.

I am unresolved on the question of how deep the differences ultimately run, but possibly the placial contrasts might be helpful in answering this question. Arguably, for Basil and the Gregories, human concepts involve the circumscription of a perimeter around a discrete quantity. Perhaps a parallel can be drawn between this way of locating human thought, and the fact that Nyssen, at least, uses evocative language to depict three divine persons whirling around each other. It is possible, further, that this way of locating the persons might strike different chord than that struck by Augustine; who at points seems to imagine conceptual thought as having to do more with the generation a mental picture of a thing rather than with tracing its perimeter. And perhaps these differences further dictate a meaningful difference in trinitarian sensibility—between a dynamic and relational Cappadocian model, and a more fixed Augustinian model.

What I want to highlight, though, is the way in which the aforementioned examples of patristic trinitarian thought are all place-freighted. Placial language informs the trinitarian descriptors, even while it also designates what cannot be the case (an intervalized trinity, a spatially distended deity). Place also frames the epistemological problems that come when one attempts to describe God. We cannot draw a delimiting boundary around God; nor can we manufacture an inner mental representation of God in our intellects, which we then presume to relate to in the manner of a creator relating to something within his or her realm. To do so, and to call the result "God," is indeed an idolatrous maneuver. It posits oneself and one's own intellect as that which truly measures all things in the cosmos; and it is to worship one's own artifact as divine.

Yet crucially, idolatry is not the *only* association that place has in these texts, if we admit instances of placial language as data points. For place in fact abounds, in ways that seem perhaps especially to resonate in discussions of pneumatology. So although place is not thematized in a way that squares with contemporary place studies, neither is it quite the problem that it seems to be for the two contemporary trinitarian theologians I have discussed: Jean-Luc Marion and Jürgen Moltmann.

Contemporary Worries and Appropriations

In considering the relative merits of Moltmann and Marion, one interpretation rather immediately suggests itself, and it would run thus: Despite their differences, both the Cappadocians and Augustine exhibit a profound

The Place of the Spirit

allergy toward conceiving God in terms of space. This allergy reveals a fundamental patristic *refusal* of any place for God. Again and again and again it is emphasized: God is not placed. If such an affirmation runs us into theological difficulty, if it seems as though we are going to have to affirm that God is placed, then that very difficulty must mark limits of human thought about God—for whatever else may be true, God cannot be placed. Thus (the thinking would run) Marion is a faithful exponent of the patristic view. For there is little which Marion emphasizes more than the refusal of God to show up within a horizon; indeed, the main conceptual work performed by paternal-filial distance is to encode, in God, a refusal to be present within any set of conditions whatsoever. By contrast, Moltmann (again, following this line of thinking) fails because he tries too incautiously to bring God into horizons: first history, and in recent years space.

In my opinion such an interpretation is defensible, but ultimately fails to take account of the complexities of place. For Marion to win the day, and Moltmann to lose, then place must end up meaning what Marion has it mean—but this is difficult to square with what the patristic authors have implied through their willingness to use place language. So the question becomes, what does place mean, for Marion and for Moltmann? And is this symptomatic, perhaps, of a more widespread contemporary distortion? I suggest this is the case. Place—understood to exceed simple corporeal location, and having to do primarily with the intelligibility and symbolic navigability of locales for human creatures—may not have showed up as a full-fledged area of inquiry in the fourth century. Neither, though, did space function as a metaphor for any set of conditions to which God's relationship is contestable. That is to say, spatial exteriority had not achieved master status as the figure for God's alterity; nor had spatial interiority achieved master status as metaphor for God being here with us. Indeed, all of the patristic authors I have treated here evidently agreed that spatialized interiority and exteriority were not the point. If God is not omnipresent by being extended everywhere throughout creation, then surely God's alterity need not involve God's evacuating any created horizon. Yet that choice, I think, frames the contemporary trinitarian models far more than the patristic ones.

To be clear, I do not mean to suggest that either Marion or Moltmann subscribe to a crudely material understanding of God—one who is either physically inside creation and needs to be gotten out, or physically outside creation and needs to be gotten in. Rather, I suggest that for both authors, the spatialized, domain-centric understanding of location has been allowed to disrupt (in Moltmann's case) or overreach (in Marion's) their trinitarian reflections. In each case, the problematic assumption sneaks in so early that its unsuitability fails to announce itself.

For in fact, Marion and Moltmann are considering a central theological question not at all foreign to that considered by Augustine, Basil, Nazianzen and Nyssen. That question might be somewhat woodenly put like this: "In order for God to be truly other than us and not a creature, God has to be somewhere else; but in order for us to know God and for God to act toward us, God has to be here. How can this be?" The problem with the contemporary answers is, as I see it, twofold. First, "outside," "somewhere else," and "here" tend to become implicitly spatial where they ought to have remained placial. Divine exteriority, for example, comes to connote a shrugging off of any attempt at delimitation or containment; any sense of being coextensive with or overlapping with anything other than itself; and/or an inaccessibility to knowledge.

So one part of the task is to appropriately designate what we are talking about when we talk about exteriority and interiority in relation to God, God's triunity, and God's relationship to creation. Marion, for one, tends to forget that exteriority and interiority are first and foremost place concepts; and that it may be appropriate to let them remain so. Before they are employed as metaphors for ontology, history, horizons, creation, etc., exteriority and interiority are about the human task of navigating environments. Place becomes, accordingly, shrouded. Moltmann does a bit better in this regard, for at least he thematizes place. I think, though, that Moltmann neglects an important element of place. When we talk about place, we are talking—just as surely as if the topic were conceptual thought—about ways in which human creatures navigate, make intelligible, the environments they find themselves in. That is the creaturely domain from which interiority and exteriority are derived.

This need not remove God from the picture, however, any more than a general discussion of intelligibility need remove God from the picture. For notice again how easy it is to use this understanding of navigability in a faithfully (if idiosyncratically) Augustinian way. If, with Augustine, we imagine God as the light of truth by which humans see and generate concepts, we may easily extend this further and imagine God as the light of truth by which we navigate and structure environments. And we may say, further, that the human ability to locate an intelligible world itself refers to—without straightforwardly locating—a creating God whose triune activity is somehow manifested in the inhabitability of creation. Nor is such a spinoff difficult to accomplish on the Cappadocian side. Basil's meditation upon the Spirit as place; Nazianzen's metaphor of God as a thoughtful arranger of a navigable cosmos; and Nyssen's connection of human conceptual circumscription with an image of trinitarian peripheries . . . All of these allow human place making to function as a necessary aspect of human knowing, which therefore reflects something of who God is even while not exhaustively locating who God is. Moreover, they suggest possibilities for placially rich accounts of the trinitarian economy, which could then veer into considerations of the trinity "ad intra" without risking either incoherence or dual trinities. One simply would say that human beings are creatures for whom intelligibility requires placial navigability; and therefore, when we speak in ways that put God somewhere else, or designate some aspect of God which we can never approach or see, it is a way of speaking required by creaturehood.

But is this possible for Marion? Frankly, I do not see how. Marion, so concerned to avoid idolatry, so careful about not having metaphysics situate God, has another concern which trips him up here. Certainly, the subjective, experiential aspects of place would do little to help alleviate Marion's worries about Hegel—and specifically his worries about a Hegelian eliding of Spirit and human subjectivity.[5] Yet place, as I have been using it, *is* about human subjectivity; and moreover, a trinitarian consideration of place seems to suggest pneumatology rather quickly. Perhaps Marion can best be understood as protecting God—rather misguidedly so, in my opinion—by not allowing human place-making to gain any access, for fear that it delimit God, making God into a delimited, finite, fully present artifact of the human activity of place-making. And doubtless there are ways in which Marion is also sticking closely to Levinas here. Levinas, while not exactly anxious about subjectivity per se, is certainly concerned to avoid the reduction of the Other to the gaze in which it shows up. The face-to-face encounter in Levinas, which Marion draws deeply from in (among other places) "The Intentionality of Love," exhibits this similar sort of placed placelessness: the Other's gaze has a priority exceeding any condition or location I might impose upon it; yet the resulting ethics are placed in terms of "above," "below" and *u-topos*, place-out-of-place, in which care is enacted. In any case, the end result is that, for Marion, the human faculty of

5. O'Regan, "Jean-Luc Marion: Crossing Hegel," 95–150.

place making loses its ability to refer to or reflect anything about who God is—even though, presumably, it is this God who made human creatures. By steering so sharply clear of Hegel; by working so hard to think God as an Other "outside" of my totalizing gaze; and by agreeing with Levinas that "[t]his unusual outside is not another landscape,"[6] Marion may have accomplished many things, but this one thing is sacrificed. Experiential, human world structuring cannot have anything to do with who God is. To say otherwise flirts too dangerously with idolatry, comes too close to adopting a totalizing gaze.

Ironically, this worry actually gives cover to the *spatialized* understanding of exteriority. Uniform space—objective, capacious, possibly infinite, punctuate, delimiting, not corralled by any one subject or perspective. In many respects, as pointed out by Casey and others, this understanding of space is the placial realization of metaphysics. Tuan counts it as mythical, an abstraction posited in order that the rest of our navigations make sense. Heidegger and Bachelard rail against it. How is it that it sneaks in to an ostensibly post-metaphysical discussion of Father, Son, and Spirit? In my opinion, though I think this would need to be explored more in depth, the allergy to human subjectivity is the culprit. Perhaps my point can best be gotten at by asking what category of location suggests itself, if one is primarily concerned not to give human subjectivity any toehold? Is it place or space? Place acknowledges its subjective constitution; by definition, it consists of the dynamic activity of subjects finding themselves within worlds and then rendering them navigable.

But space—as abstraction—extrapolates from individual perspectives. Could this account for Marion's rather startling willingness to use "interiority" and "exteriority" in ways that seem more spatial than placial, even though to do so tends to invokes the very totalizing constructs he seeks to avoid? Could it be that Marion's exit strategy from within "the Marches of Metaphysics" runs into trouble because ultimately he seeks an "outside" that is non-perspectival and objective . . . and thus shows him to be using a spatial calculus similar to the one used within the marches? At this point, I can only say that I find it possible. To make the case thoroughly, I think one would have to look more carefully at Marion as a reader of Descartes, comparing his reading of Descartes to that of Bachelard, Heidegger, and Levinas. Moreover, one would need to do so with a particular eye to place and space: how (if at all) they are thematized, and under what

---

6. Drabinski, "Wealth and Justice in a U-Topian Context," 188.

The Place of the Spirit

conditions, and to what end, and admitting what level of subjectivity or perspective. I have not been able to accomplish that in this dissertation, not least because it would have carried me too far from the topic of Marion's explicitly theological work—which is my ground for including him in a dissertation along with Augustine, Basil, the Gregories, and Moltmann. But based on my reading of his early works, I feel somewhat confident about where the answer would likely be located. And based on those works, I do think it possible that Marion has allowed an ontotheological understanding of space to determine his critique of ontotheology. At least, I do not see that this criticism can be easily ruled out.

But what of Moltmann? For starters, as I discussed in chapter three, there are several snapshots of Moltmann that one does well to consider separately. The early Moltmann is particularly concerned with history as the horizon from which God has been too far exiled and into which God has got to be re-invited. The middle Moltmann attempts to anchor his reflections more firmly in the trinity—first with respect to history, but more recently turning to space, place, and ecology Moltmann has thereby been able to imagine the Holy Spirit as a "broad place" from within which the church worships, prays, and conducts theology. The connection to epistemology, in turn, becomes explicit in *Experiences in Theology: Ways and Forms of Christian Theology*. There he affirms a kind of asymmetry, but it is different from the one I see in the patristic sources. True, for Moltmann, God is known as God by human knowers who are very different from God—yet this very ability of human knowers to know actually shows God to be indwelling in creatures. In the end, however, I think that Moltmann's dialectical emphasis also serves to privilege space over place. My best guess is that space sneaks in, and place gets crowded out, through rather a different mechanism than it does in Marion's work. For Marion, the issue was his allergy to subjectivity, and especially subjectivity colluding with pneumatology in anything like a Hegelian fashion. Suffice it to say this is not the worry for Moltmann. In Moltmann's early work, by contrast, space early on sneaks in under the guise of emptiness and not-God. One of the criticisms leveled against Moltmann throughout his career is that he requires God to realize godself as God, by overcoming alienation and taking what is other than God into godself. I cannot say whether this is characteristic Moltmann's project across the board, at all points in his career. I do feel somewhat confident in saying that it situates his early theological implications for space and place. As I've already discussed in chapter three, there remain hints of this even in

Trinity and the Kingdom, written after Moltmann has attempted to ameliorate some of the criticisms of *Theology of Hope*. Indeed, it almost seems as though the use of divine self-restriction is a spatial answer to the criticism that *Theology of Hope* had intervalized the trinity in history. The attempted remedies—perichoresis and ecology—stand in uneasy tension, throughout Moltmann's middle and later work, with restriction.

In appropriating Moltmann's insight for a future trinitarian theology of place, therefore, I shall find it most helpful to draw upon *God in Creation*, especially the chapter on space and its emphasis on ecology, dwelling, and interconnectivity. But I shall not situate it within a dialectical structure of the sort Moltmann prefers. Rather, I shall situate place and space as an aspect of intelligibility—and from there, follow both the patristic guides as well as the placial advocates; all while heeding Marion's appropriate warnings about metaphysical idolatry, albeit not remedying them in the way he chooses.

Perhaps for sentimental reasons, I conclude my dissertation hoping that the alternative I've begun to offer is more Augustinian and Cappadocian than Heideggerian. I realize, however, that that may not be the case—and at any rate will require a subsequent volume to tease out. The theological picture I am trying to paint, is a picture of human knowers who are place-makers: those who navigate the cosmos, build environments, make up stories about what lies beyond their familiar terrain, and give symbolic meaning to "up," "down," and "center." My intention is not to give this faculty exhaustive scope. I intend, rather, to build in protections against the very understandable worry—shared by many of my interlocutors—that human faculties can so easily slide into idolatry. Yet I am not willing to count human place making as theologically inappropriate or unimportant. Realizing how fraught such a move can be, and with the patristic thinkers as my models, I suggest that human creatures' placial faculties reflect and derive from God's triune activity toward creation. We find ourselves within this reality, yet we find ourselves also overlaying meaningful structures upon the reality we find ourselves in. Moreover, both of these discoveries are articulated by means of placial language and concepts. Does this mean that we locate God straightforwardly? No; nor does it mean that there is some realm called "place" or "space" in relation to which God can once and for all be mapped.

Place connects to trinitarian thought by way of the economy. To put it rather clumsily, if a triune God has created us as placial knowers—as creatures who navigate and locate as a part of making creation intelligible—then perhaps we ought to expect that our encounter with God's triunity, faltering and impartial though it may be, will suggest concepts of a God who is placed. Or even a God who is place, where the "is" functions non-predicatively. I have suggested one way of imagining this which draws particularly upon Basil and Augustine: that we can imagine the Spirit as being a bit like a place, inasmuch as we are accustomed to thinking of ourselves being in the Spirit even while the Spirit dwells in us. This is not altogether strange, because in fact the way place works generally could be understood to derive from how the Spirit acts. It is not unusual to find that being-indwelled-by and dwelling-within happen together . . . if, that is, we attend to how place actually works rather than focus on describing a pre-constituted spatial domain. But back to the trinitarian metaphor: we could, I suggested, take it even further, and imagine the Spirit locating the reciprocal beholding and representing of the Father and the Son in love. This metaphor need not demote the Spirit or threaten the Spirit's agency, provided we understand what we mean by place. Bachelard's childhood house is no passive expanse, no derivative interval. So these possibilities arise for thinking place in conjunction with trinitarian thought. However, they only do so if one is careful about one's understanding of place, admitting more than just physical extension, and guarding against a totalizing modern conception of space which has a way of sneaking itself in.

To run with the image of Spirit as place, is simply to note that what we understand of the Spirit's activity tends to evoke the mutuality, the simultaneous beholding and representing, that we notice in our own activity of place making. It is also to note—as I have noted throughout—that conversations about place, and God, seem very quickly to become pneumatological. Nevertheless, I intend to herald all of this with the most Augustinian of disclaimers: that in no case ought we plot God according to our own placial coordinates, and that if my pneumatological metaphor does not work one should feel free to toss it out. My overriding concern here is to argue that it is not improper to, prudently and judiciously, use place language about God, provided we understand what we are doing when we do so. Beyond just not being inappropriate, in fact the theological advantages of doing this work abound. We are given resources for explaining what we mean when say that God dwells, or that God is inside, or that God is outside. We can consider more deeply the important theological work performed by metaphors of ascent, of looking inward, of mentally circumscribing. We are not left trying to disguise an ontologically questionable expanse which has sneaked its way into our theological model, subtly determining all the rules about what God has to be protected from and what God has to be able to relate to. Nor are we left trying to account for an understanding of place that seems a theological non sequitur, having nothing to do with God, but already assumed in any discussion of creation. On the theological anthropology front—which I find myself, at the end of this dissertation, most intrigued by—we now have another angle from which to consider how human knowing reflects the God who created human knowers. Moreover, this particular angle opens up possibilities for fruitful dialogue with scholars and practitioners in human geography, sociology, and even architecture. Particularly as economic pressures and emerging technologies move some churches move into new kinds of built environments, a trinitarian lens may prove useful.

And, indeed, I hope that the case I am making might be a fruitful addition to those advocacies already undertaken in Moltmann's and Marion's work. A trinitarian theology of place should have something to say about the ever-present temptation to build idols to ourselves in public spaces; and it should have something to say about the self-destructive entitlement with which human beings have helped themselves to whatever resources they could yank from the cosmos. One possible fault with my project, as I've laid it out so far, is that it is fairly optimistic about human place-making—more dazzled by the mutuality and creativity that occurs between humans and environments, and less concerned about what happens when such creativity becomes devastatingly self-serving. I admit this with some surprise, seeing as I have understood myself to be taking cues from Augustine. Therefore, as I develop this project in future books, I expect that I shall continue to draw heavily from Augustine, Marion, and Moltmann. They have certainly proven challenging and edifying guides thus far, and my navigation here has only left me with more to explore.

Bibliography

Anderson, David. "Introduction." In *St. Basil the Great, on the Holy Spirit*. Crestwood, NY: St. Vladimir's Seminary Press, 1997.
Anderson, David. *St. Basil the Great On the Holy Spirit*. Crestwood, NY: St. Vladimir's Seminary Press, 1997.
Augustine. *The Confessions*. Translated by Maria Boulding. New York: Vintage, 1998.
———. *The Trinity: De Trinitate*. Translated by Edmund Hill. Edited by John E. Rotelle. The Works of Saint Augustine: A Translation for the 21st Century 5. Brooklyn, NY: New City, 1991.
Ayres, Lewis. *Augustine and the Trinity*. New York: Cambridge University Press, 2010.
———. *Nicaea and Its Legacy: An Approach to Fourth-Century Trinitarian Theology*. Oxford: Oxford University Press, 2004.
———. "On Not Three People: The Fundamental Themes of Gregory of Nyssa's Trinitarian Theology as Seen in 'to Ablabius: On Not Three Gods.'" *Modern Theology* 18.4 (2002) 445–74.
Bachelard, Gaston. *The Philosophy of No: A Philosophy of the New Scientific Mind*. Translated by G. C. Waterston. New York: Orion, 1968.
———. *The Poetics of Space: The Classic Look at How We Experience Intimate Places*. Translated by Maria Jolas. Boston: Beacon, 1969.
Bauckham, Richard. *The Theology of Jürgen Moltmann*. London: T. & T. Clark, 1995.
Beeley, Christopher A. *Gregory of Nazianzus on the Trinity and the Knowledge of God: In Your Light We See Light*. Oxford: Oxford University Press, 2008.
Bernasconi, Robert. "The Face of the Other: A Review of the Work of Emmanuel Levinas." *Religious Studies Review* 16.3 (1990) 227–32.
Bobrinskoy, Boris. "The Indwelling of the Spirit of Christ: 'Pneumatic Christology' in the Cappadocian Fathers." *St Vladimir's Theological Quarterly* 28.1 (1984) 49–65.
Brockelman, Thomas. "Lost in Place? On the Virtues and Vices of Edward Casey's Anti-Modernism." *Humanitas* 16.1 (2003) 36–37.
Caputo, John D. "Heidegger and Theology." In *The Cambridge Companion to Heidegger*, edited by Charles B. Guignon. New York: Cambridge University Press, 1993.
Caputo, John D., and Michael J. Scanlon. *God, the Gift, and Postmodernism*. Edited by John D. Caputo and Michael J. Scanlon. Bloomington: Indiana University Press, 1999.
Cary, Phillip. *Augustine's Invention of the Inner Self: The Legacy of a Christian Platonist*. Oxford: Oxford University Press, 2000.
Casey, Edward. *The Fate of Place: A Philosophical History*. Berkeley: University of California Press, 1997.
Cavadini, John C. "The Darkest Enigma: Reconsidering the Self in Augustine's Thought." *Augustinian Studies* 38.1 (2007) 119–32.
Cavadini, John C. "Review of *Augustine's Invention of the Inner Self* by Phillip Cary." *Modern Theology* 18.3 (2002) 425–28.

Bibliography

Derrida, Jacques. *Margins of Philosophy*. Chicago: University of Chicago Press, 1982.

Descartes, René. *Descartes: Philosophical Letters*. Translated by Anthony Kenny. Oxford: Clarendon, 1970.

———. "Meditations on First Philosophy." In *Descartes: Key Philosophical Writings*, translated by Elizabeth S. Haldane and G. R. T. Ross, 170–72. Ware, England: Wordsworth, 1997.

———. *Principles of Philosophy*. Translated with explanatory notes by Valentine Rodger Miller and Reese P. Miller. Boston: Kluwer, 1983.

———. "Rules for the Direction of the Mind." In *The Philosophical Works of Descartes*, translated by Elizabeth Sanderson Haldane and G. R. T. Ross, vol 1. London, England: Cambridge University Press, 1973.

Drabinski, John. "Wealth and Justice in a U-Topian Context." In *Addressing Levinas*, edited by Eric Sean Nelson, Antje Kapust and Kent Still. Evanston, IL: Northwestern University Press, 2005.

Garber, Daniel. "Descartes, René." *Routledge Encyclopedia of Philosophy* (1998, 2003). Online: http://www.rep.routledge.com/article/DA026.

Gelven, Michael. *A Commentary on Heidegger's Being and Time: A Section-by-Section Interpretation*. New York: Harper & Row, 1970.

Guignon, Charles B. *The Cambridge Companion to Heidegger*. New York: Cambridge University Press, 1993.

Hardy, Edward Rochie. *Christology of the Later Fathers*. The Library of Christian Classics. Louisville: Westminster John Knox, 1954.

Heidegger, Martin. *Being and Time*. Translated by John Macquarrie and Edward Robinson. New York: Harper, 1962.

Heidegger, Martin. "Building, Dwelling, Thinking." In *Rethinking Architecture: A Reader in Cultural Theory*, edited by Neil Leach. New York: Routledge, 1997.

———. *An Introduction to Metaphysics*. Translated by Ralph Manheim. New Haven: Yale University Press, 1959.

———. "The Nature of Language." In *On the Way to Language*. New York: Harper & Row, 1971.

———. "The Origin of the Work of Art." In *Poetry, Language, Thought*, 55. New York: Harper & Row, 1971.

———. "The Thing." In *Poetry, Language, Thought*, 165. New York: Harper & Row, 1971.

———. "Time and Being." In *On Time and Being*. New York: Harper & Row, 1969.

Horner, Robyn. *Rethinking God as Gift: Marion, Derrida, and the Limits of Phenomenology*. New York: Fordham University Press, 2001.

Husserl, Edmund. *The Crisis of European Sciences and Transcendental Phenomenology*. Translated by D. Carr. Evanston: Northwestern University Press, 1970.

Kisiel, Theodore. *Genesis of Heidegger's Being and Time*. Berkeley: University of California Press, 1993.

LaCugna, Catherine Mowry. *God for Us: The Trinity and Christian Life*. San Francisco: HarperSanFrancisco, 1991.

Lévinas, Emmanuel. *Difficult Freedom: Essays on Judaism*. Baltimore: Johns Hopkins University Press, 1990.

Marion, Jean-Luc. *God without Being*. Translated by Thomas A. Carlson. Chicago: University of Chicago Press, 1991.

———. *The Idol and Distance: Five Studies*. Translated by Thomas A. Carlson. New York: Fordham University Press, 2001.

Bibliography

———. *Prolegomena to Charity*. Translated by Stephen E. Lewis. New York: Fordham University Press, 2002.
McDougall, Joy Ann. *Pilgrimage of Love: Moltmann on the Trinity and Christian Life*. Reflection and Theory in the Study of Religion. Oxford: Oxford University Press, 2005.
Meeks, M. Douglas. *Origins of the Theology of Hope*. Philadelphia: Fortress, 1974.
Miller, Isaac. "Idolatry and the Polemics of World-Formation from Philo to Augustine." *Journal of Religious History* 28.2 (2004) 126–45.
Moltmann, Jürgen. *The Coming of God: Christian Eschatology*. Minneapolis: Fortress, 1996.
———. *Experiences in Theology: Ways and Forms of Christian Theology*. Minneapolis: Fortress, 2000.
———. *God in Creation: A New Theology of Creation and the Spirit of God*. Translated by Margaret Kohl. Minneapolis: Fortress, 1993.
———. *Theology of Hope*. Minneapolis: Fortress, 1993.
———. *The Trinity and the Kingdom*. Minneapolis: Fortress, 1993.
Moran, Dermot. *Introduction to Phenomenology*. London: Routledge, 2000.
Narkevics, Edgars, "Skiagraphia: Outlining the conception of God in Gregory's Theological Orations." In *Gregory of Nazianzus: Images and Reflections*, edited by J. Børtnes and T. Hägg. Copenhagen: Museum Tusculanum, 2006.
O'Regan, Cyril. "Jean-Luc Marion: Crossing Hegel." In *Counter-Experiences: Reading Jean-Luc Marion*, edited by Kevin Hart, 95–150. Notre Dame, IN: University of Notre Dame Press, 2007.
Pelikan, Jaroslav. *Christianity and Classical Culture: The Metamorphosis of Natural Theology in the Christian Encounter with Hellenism*. New Haven: Yale University Press, 1993.
Relph, Edward. "Disclosing the Ontological Depth of Place: *Heidegger's Topology* by Jeff Malpas." *Environmental and Architectural Phenomenology Newsletter* 19.1 (2008) 5.
Schaff, Philip, and Henry Wace. *A Select Library of Nicene and Post-Nicene Fathers of the Christian Church Second Series*. Translated by Blomfield Jackson. 8 vols. Grand Rapids: Eerdmans. Online, via Christian Classics Ethereal Library, Calvin College: http://www.ccel.org/ccel/schaff/npnf208.viii.ii.html.
Stramara, Daniel F. "Gregory of Nyssa's Terminology for Trinitarian Perichoresis." *Vigiliae Christianae* 52.3 (1998) 257–63.
Taylor, Charles. *Sources of the Self: The Making of the Modern Identity*. Cambridge: Harvard University Press, 1989.
Tiles, Mary. *Bachelard: Science and Objectivity*. Cambridge: Cambridge University Press, 1984.
Tuan, Yi-Fu. "Dear Colleague." Vol. 5, no. 10 (1990). Online: http://www.yifutuan.org/archive/1990/19900115.pdf.
———. *Space and Place: The Perspective of Experience*. Minneapolis: University of Minnesota Press, 1977.
———. *Topophilia: A Study of Environmental Perception, Attitudes, and Values*. Englewood Cliffs, NJ: Prentice-Hall, 1974.
Tuan, Yi-fu, and Martha Strawn. *Religion: From Place to Placelessness*. Chicago: Center for American Places at Columbia College Chicago: Distributed by the University of Chicago Press, 2009.

Bibliography

Verghese, Paul T. "*Diastema* and *Diastasis* in Gregory of Nyssa: Introduction to a Concept and the Posing of a Problem." In *Gregor von Nyssa und Die Philosophie: zweites internationales Kolloquium über Gregor von Nyssa, Freckenhorst bei Münster 18–23 September 1972*, edited by Heinrich Dörrie, Margarete Altenburger, and Uta Schramm. Leiden: Brill, 1976.

Zizioulas, John. *Being as Communion: Studies in Personhood and the Church*. Crestwood, NY: St. Vladimir's Seminary Press, 1997.